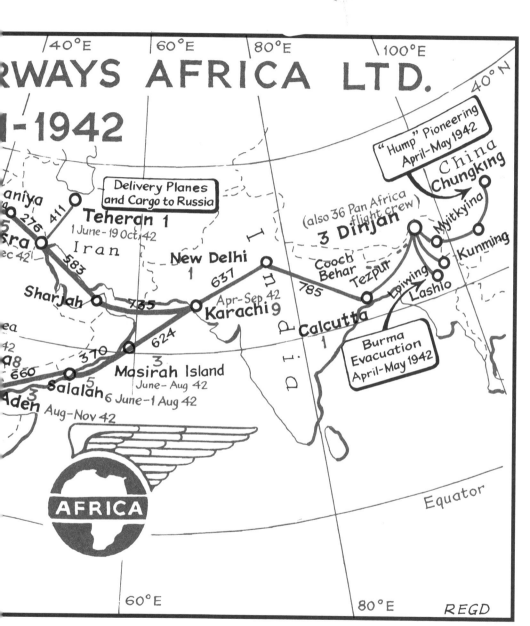

PanAfrica

Across the Sahara in 1941 with Pan Am

Tom Culbert & Andy Dawson

Paladwr Press

To all the intrepid aviators and steadfast ground support personnel, who worked together to establish the foundations of a modern aviation system in Africa. They experienced the thrills and endured the hardships associated with aviation pioneering on the vast and magnificent African continent. They did their jobs well.

Fourth printing, 2007

Copyright © 1998 by
Tom Culbert, Andy Dawson, and Paladwr Press

All rights reserved. No part of this book may be
reproduced or transmitted in any form or by any
means, electronic or mechanical including photo-
copying, recording or by any information storage
and retrieval system, without permission from
the holders of the copyright.

Published 1998 by Paladwr Press,
1906 Wilson Lane, Apt. 101, McLean, Virginia
22102-1957

Manufactured in the United States

Maps by R.E.G. Davies

Edited by R.E.G. Davies

Typesetting/Layout by Spot Color Incorporated

ISBN 978-0-88896-212-6

Contents

Exhibits

The map that comprises the endpapers of this book was drawn by R.E.G. Davies, and based on detailed information that was assembled by co-author Andy Dawson from fellow members of the PAA-Africa Alumni Association

Foreword

In September 1943, as a young Army Air Force second lieutenant three months out of flying school, I boarded a Pan American Airways DC-4, headed east out of Miami. I did not know where we were going, 2nd Lieutenants are not supposed to know much, but I suspected it would be the China Burma India theater because I was a P-40 pilot and that was the only theater where they were still in use. I was lucky to be on this airplane as it was carrying the new ambassador to China and his staff so we had regular airliner seats instead of the military bucket seats.

We flew the standard South Atlantic route: Borinquén Field, Puerto Rico; Georgetown, British Guiana; Belém and Natal, Brazil; Ascension Island; Accra, Gold Coast; Maiduguri, Nigeria; French Equatorial Africa; Khartoum, Anglo-Egyptian Sudan; Aden; and Karachi, India. Along with several other junior birdmen, I left the plane in Karachi, where we were to receive further training before going into combat in China.

I had no knowledge of the importance of that South Atlantic trans-Africa route or of its fascinating history until I read *Pan Africa: Across the Sahara in 1941 with Pan Am.* Late in 1940 the British were heavily engaged in North Africa and were finding it difficult to supply their troops because of the German forces in the Mediterranean and the Atlantic. They were looking to the air route across Africa to deliver supplies and ferry aircraft to the combat areas. The British Imperial Airways service from West Africa was equipped only with small de Havilland aircraft types; and thus the shortage of their own aircraft and aircrews hampered the British attempt to meet the challenge of distance, terrain, and lack of suitable airfields. They asked for assistance from the United States and Pan American Airways.

The U. S. Army Air Corps flew a test mission across the South Atlantic trans-Africa route and confirmed its practicality and future value. Accordingly, in mid-July, Pan American formed two new subsidiaries, Pan American Airways-Africa, Ltd. and Pan American Air Ferries, Inc. These new companies were to fly Lend-Lease airplanes to their final destination in Africa using facilities provided and manned by Pan Am Africa. Airplanes and supplies were delivered to the British in Africa and to the Flying Tigers in China eliminating the long dangerous sea voyages. When the Japanese victories in Burma closed the only land supply line into China, a number of the Pan Am crews were diverted to India, where, despite inadequate equipment and facilities, initiated the air supply line to China over the Himalayan mountains—known as The Hump. In 1942, with the United States now in the war, the Army Air Forces began to work with Pan Am to expand the airlift capability of the entire route to satisfy the increased demands. The AAF gradually took over the operation of the entire U.S. to China route and in December 1942 the Pan Am contract was terminated and the military assumed full control. Many Pan Am Africa employees accepted commissions in the AAF and remained in their old jobs.

Despite its relatively short existence, Pan Am Africa made significant contributions to the war effort. The routes it established and developed became the key to carrying on the war against the Japanese in China. In fact, it demonstrated the importance of organized airlift and led directly to the formation of the Air Transport Command. Its post-war impact was significant also as many of the airfields it developed are now major commercial airports.

Pan Africa has all the attributes of a good book. It is informative, clearly presenting a great deal of interesting history that is not well known, without being pedantic. It is well written with a straightforward narrative style, liberally sprinkled with anecdotal material, humorous and otherwise. The occasional conflicts that arose between Pan Am and the British and later between Pan Am and the USAAF are covered in an even-handed manner without bias. The illustrations are well chosen and add greatly to the narrative. The maps are excellent and are a great help in clarifying what is unfamiliar territory to most of us. *Pan Africa* is a valuable addition to the history of World War II.

Don Lopez
Deputy Director
National Air and Space Museum

Authors' Preface

The genesis of this project to document the history of Pan American Airways-Africa Ltd. (PAA-Africa) had two diverse starting points.

In August 1979, Air Force Captain Tom Culbert arrived at the U.S. Embassy in Cairo as the Assistant Air Force Attaché in Egypt. One of his primary duties was to establish flight operations and to serve as the lead pilot for the newly-assigned USAF C-12 aircraft. During his three years in Cairo, he made many flights, carrying VIPs throughout northeastern Africa and the Middle East and frequenting most of the larger airfields in the region. Some airfields, such as El Fasher and El Obeid in western Sudan, began to puzzle him. He asked, "Why did these airfields exist in such desolate regions of the African continent?" Initially, he heard some general comments that they had played a role in the Second World War as British airstrips used to support airlift and ferry operations in their fight against the Germans in north Africa.

In 1987 Tom returned to Africa for another tour of Embassy Duty, this time as a Lt. Col. Air Force Attaché based in Abidjan, Côte d'Ivoire. As a pilot, he began to see and use other major airports located in western and central Africa. These included Roberts Field in Liberia; Accra and Takoradi in Ghana; Lagos, Kano, and Maiduguri in Nigeria; and N'Djamena in Chad. The same question came to his mind, "Why are these airports located here?" The answer was provided by a British Military Attaché—they were established by the British during the War.

But something did not sound quite right. What about Chad and Liberia? These would not have been part of a British air operation. What was missing from this story?

After his retirement (or privatization as he prefers to say), Tom headed to the historical archives located in the Washington D.C. area to research the matter further. Here he read documents that described the key role played by an American civilian firm, Pan American Airways-Africa Limited, to establish the operation of the trans-Africa air route in 1941–1942. The records indicated that PAA-Africa had been contracted by the United States and British governments to establish, upgrade, and operate the route to ferry combat aircraft and supplies to their wartime allies in besieged north Africa. It evolved into a remarkable story of "Yankee ingenuity," as this group of American civilians was able to overcome extreme hardships and to establish routine flight operations across Africa within weeks of being assigned to do so by the President of the United States and the Prime Minister of Great Britain.

Tom was amazed that so little had been published about the work done by PAA-Africa. He located several magazine articles, a couple of student papers (one dissertation and one thesis), and a couple of short articles written in aviation-related scholarly journals. Even in the official histories written about World War II, there was only scant mention of the work done by the civilian employees of PAA-Africa. This situation, he felt, needed to be remedied.

A solution to the problem was found almost by accident. Andy Dawson had served with PAA-Africa in Accra as a young aviation mechanic in 1942, and joined the PAA-Africa, Ltd. alumni group in 1983. The informal association had been established in 1978 by 18 ex-PAA-Africa employees. They have been meeting annually since.

Andy, together with PAA-Africa colleague, Ray Tirado, were instrumental in collecting data for a large map showing PAA-Africa's routes across Africa and India. Several months were spent compiling information and hand-drawing a 16-foot-long wall map of the route. The draft map was then redrawn to scale and printed by airline historian R.E.G. (Ron) Davies and distributed to the alumni group members at the 1996 reunion held in Charleston, South Carolina. The map acted as a catalyst, renewing interest amongst the membership and attracting additional members. Andy's next logical step was to document the history of this group.

Tom and Andy first met in 1994. Recognizing their mutual interest they began to collect evidence and to prepare for the production of a book. Andy called upon his colleagues in the Pan American Airways (PAA-Africa Ltd.) alumni group to come forward with personal recollections and memorabilia from their days in Africa. A questionnaire/survey was produced and sent out to the alumni group. More than seventy individuals responded, providing personal photographs, motion-picture film, official documents, and other pieces of memorabilia. Many of these same individuals gave financial support for the project.

Tom and Andy worked together as a team as they continued to gather information about PAA-Africa. They visited the National Archives in Washington, D.C., the Pan American Archives at the University of Miami; the Pan American Airways Historical Foundation Archives in New Jersey; the U.S. Military History Institute in Carlisle, Pennsylvania; the Smithsonian Institution's National Air and Space Museum Library in Washington; and approached many other sources searching for historical data.

The result of this dedicated effort—which, let it be said, was also a labor of love—is the story of a unique group of American civilian pioneers who served as the vanguard of the United States of America's prewar and wartime aviation efforts in Africa, the Middle East, and the China Theater. Their job was to ensure that U.S. allies could receive the aircraft and airlift support that, under the Lend-Lease agreements, were available, especially for General Montgomery's defense of Egypt against the Axis threats. These men have only recently been recognized by the U.S. government as true wartime veterans.

This unique company organization and its staff of extraordinary men were able to establish safe and efficient flight operations in one of the most hostile environments on earth. Because of their efforts, PAA-Africa began scheduled flights in Africa in October 1941, two months before the United States officially went to war. The impact went well beyond the support provided to the British forces fighting in North Africa. During its 16 months of existence, PAA-Africa's aircraft ranged as far east as China and as far north as the Soviet Union. Their support of evacuation missions ensured that hundreds of Allied soldiers and civilians were saved from capture and certain death at the hands of the Japanese army in Burma. Additionally, thousands of American combat aircraft were able to fly safely across Africa using the airports and infrastructure established by PAA-Africa. These Lend-Lease aircraft provided the vital offensive punch needed by our allies such as the Soviet Union, the Free French, Great Britain, the Netherlands, and South Africa.

We felt that this story had to be told, so here it is, warts and all.

Tom Culbert & Andy Dawson
November 1998

Publisher's Note

The publication of this book has been a great privilege for Paladwr Press. We feel that we have helped the co-authors to give long-overdue recognition to a branch of the Pan American aviation fraternity who labored almost anonymously for many months, and whose contribution to a vital Allied logistics effort was immeasurable, yet little appreciated.

Paladwr adopted the title of the book as a coined word to encapsulate the mission of PAA-Africa Ltd. Just as the term Pan American implied an aerial hegemony over the Americas, so did the hastily-organized sub-division exert an influence in Africa that was just as far-reaching. Its importance and value, both to the military forces it supported, and to the establishment of a sound aviation infrastructure across a continent, were incomparable.

R.E.G. Davies

Acknowledgments

The authors wish to extend a sincere thank you to the following individuals and organizations that have graciously provided support in the production of this book. Those listed below provided either written personal accounts, private photographic collections, audio tapes, research assistance, or monetary contributions, or a combination of these in support of this project.

Moses Acosta, Robert S. Allen, Carl Antone, Andrew Austin, Milo Bacon, Merry Herd Barton, Arthur Beaudet, Elliot A. Billings, Philip A. Brown, Richard L. Brinkerhoff, Gifford Bull, Kathleen Clair, George C. Clayton, Ernest and Scharleen Colant, Floyd H. Coverly, Dornan S. Craig, Margaret Culbert, R.E.G. "Ron" Davies, Andy Dawson, B. F. Denny, Desmond Drea, Armond Droz, Len Eagles, Thomas E. Elder, Ivan Wayne Eveland, David Farabaugh, Thomas J. Flanagan, Edward G. Frankiewicz, Dr. Voit Gilmore, Peter J. Goutiere, Thomas L. "Roy" Hackett, Grant and Norman Hayes, Charles R. Heffner, Barton Hewitt, Gordon Hill, Walter Holloway, Tom Hoopes, Jack D. Hudson, Joe Hughes, Ralph Hunt, Harry D. Jenkins, Howard Jenson, Thor Johnson, Harry J. Kardel, William D. Kent, Clarence F. "Linn" Linenbach, Paul D. Liscomb, Miller Logan, Speck Lund, Tom MacKay, Sam Marchinsky, Edward Mathwig, E.C. "Mac" McCaslin, Bill McClinchy, Edmund "Randy" McKane, Richard K. Miller, Robert H. Morrow, Roy Moungovan, Bob Nelson, Dean Newell, John T. "Pat" Passage, Joe Patrick, Lemuel Lee Payne, Philip B. Piazza, Frank V. Pierlas, Lyle Pigort, Margaret Purcell, Woods K. Rawlinson, Paul Roitsch, Matt Rodina, David Rush, James H. Schnell, Gov. William W. Scranton, Kim Scribner, Ed T. Shaffer, Bernard L. Sherwood, Dwight L. Shrum, Matt St. George, Carl Stephen, Don Stoeger, John T. "Jack" Swift, Ray Tirado, Edward A. Tobin, Ella Schoenknecht Tooles, Kinsley "Bud" Twining, Bradford B. Urmston, Thomas W. Usinger, Leo Viens, William D. Wersen, Irvin "Les" White, Jr., Harold B. Whitman Jr., Thomas J. Whittaker, Sr., L. A. Wilbrew, Leroy Wilcox, Parker C. "Peter" Wiseman, World Wings International, Inc., Wilson York, Ed Young, and the staffs of the Richter Library of the University of Miami, the Military History Institute, Carlisle Barracks, Carlisle, Pennsylvania, the Pan American Historical Foundation, the Smithsonian Institution's National Air and Space Museum, and the National Archives and Records Administration at College Park, Maryland.

A special thank you is reserved for Margaret Culbert and Louise Dawson for their unending patience and encouragement to the authors during the many hours their husbands put into this project. Without their tolerance and assistance, this project could not have been completed.

Photographic Credits

Photographs used in this publication were obtained from the private collections of members of the PAA-Africa alumni group and other individuals listed above. Other sources are indicated in the captions for the individual photographs.

Photographic duplication and copy work was accomplished by Aviation Information Research Corporation and Steve Tuttle, Photographer, both of Alexandria, Virginia.

The British War Effort in Trouble

y June 1941, the war effort of His Majesty's Government in the United Kingdom against the German Nazi regime and its Axis allies was not going well. The British were becoming more dependent on the United States for raw materials, food, and arms as the Axis partners tightened their sea and air blockades of the British homeland. Better weather and longer daylight hours of the spring of 1941 brought with it more deadly air attacks from the Germans. The only bright spot for the average man in the street in London was that the United States 77th Congress had approved the Lend-Lease Act (Public Law 11) on 11 March 1941. The prospect of receiving additional quantities of military aid from the United States was a veritable light at the end of the dark tunnel of the ongoing war.

With the French surrender to Nazi military forces in June 1940, British shipping could no longer safely use the Mediterranean Sea. Loss of access to the vital sea route eastward through the Suez Canal was a serious blow to British efforts to resupply its military forces in the Middle East and Asia. Resupply shipments had to be rerouted around the southern tip of Africa to reach the most distant outposts of the British fighting forces. It could now take months to ship supplies to the troops. As German U-Boat activity increased dramatically along the African coast, even this sea lane became increasingly dangerous for the British ships.

Early in September 1940, the Royal Air Force (R.A.F.) began searching for an alternative route to get its aircraft and supplies to the forces fighting in the northern desert west of Egypt. The long and dangerous route to Egypt, by sea around the southern tip of Africa, was not adequate for the urgent requirements of the R.A.F. In an attempt to reduce shipping time, the British Air Ministry began to move pursuit-type combat aircraft to Egypt by using a combination of both surface and air shipments. The arrangements included using cargo ships to carry crated aircraft as far as the port city of Takoradi, in the British Colony of the Gold Coast (now the independent nation of Ghana). The aircraft were reassembled by British forces at the airfield in Takoradi, and then flown to Egypt, using a rudimentary air route structure across central

Africa. They attempted to use airports that had been established late in the 1930s by the pioneering efforts of the British Imperial Airways company. The difficulties encountered in this operation were enormous and many aircraft were either lost or severely damaged in early attempts to fly this route. Even with the addition of 20 transport aircraft from the United States in the spring of 1941, the British air crews could not meet the challenges posed by the African interior. The need for a better delivery system became painfully apparent. Thus, the prospects for using long-range aviation became a topic of critical importance within the highest levels of the British Government and its Air Ministry.

Faced with the Africa dilemma, and possibly coincidentally, in June 1941, the Royal Aeronautical Society invited Pan American Airways President Juan Terry Trippe to London to give the annual Wright Brothers Lecture. Trippe, who traveled to London aboard one of his Boeing B-314 Clippers, lectured on "Ocean Flying." Lord Brabazon, the chairman of the Brabazon Committee which prepared the blueprint for postwar British civil aircraft production, hosted the dinner event. Trippe's presentation that evening was

Juan Trippe
(President, Pan American Airways) The PAA-Africa route, and Pan American Airways' promotion of it, was first discussed in London when Juan Trippe met Winston Churchill in the summer of 1941. (This picture was taken after the war, as he boarded a Stratocruiser.)

apparently received very well. Immediately following the dinner, Trippe was invited by several members of the Air Ministry staff who heard his lecture to visit the Air Ministry's underground bunker, which served as the command center for coordinating British air defense efforts in the Battle of Britain.

The discussions that evening centered on the type of equipment the British might use to conduct resupply operations to Africa by air. During the course of the evening, Trippe reportedly mentioned that an efficiently-run air route, passing through central Africa and using modern equipment and airline-like operations, would reduce significantly the delivery time for military equipment, particularly when compared with the sea route around the southern tip of Africa. At the end of the meeting, Trippe was taken back to his hotel, and according to his own account, was packed and actually checking out of the hotel when he received a summons to No. 10 Downing Street. There, he sat down with Prime Minister Winston Churchill for a midnight dinner and additional discussions on ways to augment the air route across Africa.

When Juan Trippe arrived back in the United States, he landed at North Beach, New York, where he found a U.S. Marine Corps aircraft waiting to transport him to Washington for a meeting with government officials. They wanted to know the specifics of how Pan American Airways (PAA) would operate a trans-African air route. While in Washington Trippe met with James Forrestal who, as Roosevelt's "Anonymous Assistant," asked Pan Am's president to delineate the requirements for such a route and to stipulate the budget required to get the job done.

Within days, representatives from the British Air Commission, the U.S. Army Air Corps, and Pan Am began contract negotiations formalizing the details pertaining to the trans-Africa air route. Talks were concluded in several weeks, but not without some difficulty. The most contentious issue was British concern over PAA's postwar access to the installations that would be constructed in wartime. During the negotiations, the British continued to introduce clauses that were intended to protect the postwar operating rights of the British civilian air carrier, British Overseas Airways Corporation. The British negotiators were very concerned over the commercial opportunities Pan American was to receive in what the British perceived as their own back yard. The British also hedged on their original commitment to obtain the necessary flight clearances from the various governmental authorities located in the colonies, protectorates, and mandated territories through which PAA's aircraft would have to pass. Although these and other contentious issues developed, they did not derail the talks. Interestingly, the cost of the project was not an issue during these contract talks, as the U.S. government had already agreed to absorb the costs.

The military situation in north Africa was becoming too critical to delay any further. Agreement was reached and five contracts were drafted covering the details of the work that would be accomplished by Pan American. (For a more detailed discussion of the negotiations, see Chapter IV, titled, "Contracts and Conflicts," of Deborah Ray's dissertation. In that chapter she compiled a well-researched account of the negotiating sessions which were held in Washington, D.C. in July–August 1941.)[See Bibliography]

On 10 August 1941, another event took place, which most certainly affected the negotiations under way in Washington, D.C. President Franklin Roosevelt and Prime Minister Winston Churchill met secretly, along with their military staffs, on board the *H.M.S. Prince of Wales* anchored just off the coast of Maine. Roosevelt and Churchill apparently addressed the military situation facing the British in north Africa during their discussions. These meetings, referred to as the "Atlantic Charter Meetings" most likely provided the venue for the final U.S. and U.K. approvals for Pan American Airways-Africa, Limited (PAA-Africa) to operate the trans-Africa air route.

The original idea was to establish a modern air route through the British-held colonies in western and central Africa. Originating on the west coast of Africa at Bathurst, Gambia, the route would proceed to Accra, in the Gold Coast (modern-day Ghana), then to Lagos, Nigeria. In Nigeria, two additional stops would be planned at Kano and Maiduguri. Proceeding to the east, one stop was planned in Fort Lamy, French Equatorial Africa (modern-day N'Djamena, Chad). From Chad, several stations would be established in the Sudan, including El Geneina, El Fasher and Khartoum. The initial plan was to terminate the route in Khartoum. The British could then fly the Lend-Lease aircraft to their final destination in Egypt. But in reality, Khartoum was never the terminus of the route, which actually split there. One leg proceeded

President Roosevelt and Prime Minister Churchill gather with their staffs on the deck of H.M.S. Prince of Wales. *Standing, left to right: Harry Hopkins; Averill H. Harriman; Admiral Ernest J. King; Gen. George C. Marshall; Rear Admiral Ross T. McIntire; Gen. Sir John Dill; Captain John R. Beardall; Admiral H. A. Stark; Admiral Sir Dudley Pound. (National Archives)*

north, following the Nile River to Cairo. In Cairo the aircraft could land at one
of several airfields in the vicinity of the city. The second leg continued east
from Khartoum, passing through Eritrea and ending in India.

Although the original purpose for establishing the route was to assist
the British, the U.S. Army Air Corps became increasingly interested in the
benefits of establishing an African air route. The Air Corps was being asked
to increase its world-wide flight operations to support expanding requirements to fly government VIPs around the globe. The Air Corps' 10th Ferry
Squadron, Ferrying Command, launched a survey mission in August 1941 to
test the feasibility of flying across Africa. Lt. Colonel Caleb V. Haynes and
Major Curtis E. LeMay flew a B-24 from Washington, D.C., to Cairo, via the
South Atlantic and the trans-Africa route. They successfully completed the
mission and confirmed, for the U.S. Army Air Corps, the availability of a
year-round air route to the European and Middle East Theaters of war. Lt. Col.
Haynes and his crew received the Distinguished Flying Cross (DFC) for this
"pioneering flight." Haynes reappears in the PAA-Africa story in April 1942
as the Commander of the Burma evacuation operation, which will be covered
in a later chapter.

The 10th Ferry Squadron used the air route across the South Atlantic
and through central Africa for a second time later in August 1941. First Lieutenant Louis T. Reichers, piloting another B-24, used the West Africa route to
return to the United States from Moscow. Lieutenant Reichers was part of a
two-aircraft mission supporting the official visit of Averell Harriman to
Moscow for talks with Joseph Stalin.

The U.S. Army Air Corps was now convinced that the African air route
was an important link in its ability to support future mission requirements.
U.S. Army pilots had flown the route and seen it first-hand. They had noted
its potential as a supply lifeline for the allies of the United States. At the same
time they also observed the serious deficiencies of the route, especially the
lack of modern-day aviation infrastructure. Landing fields for larger aircraft,
radio communications, navigational facilities, maintenance facilities, etc.,
would all have to be in place before the route could play a more viable role in
the war effort.

By mid-summer of 1941, the stage was set for governmental action.
Juan Trippe was poised to launch an all-out effort to support the British and
the U.S. governments' requirements for a trans-Africa air route. Committed
to using all its resources, PAA-Africa prepared for large-scale flight operations on a continent virtually unknown to most Americans; a continent, which
up to this point, had seen comparatively little aviation activity. But to the

British and American governments, Africa was now looked upon as an avenue of opportunity for military forces fighting against the Axis powers.

Because of the uncertainties of wartime, the initial operational concept for this project was modified frequently by the British and the Americans. The limited scope of aviation activities, envisioned during the initial contract negotiations, were revised dramatically after the 7 December 1941 bombing of Pearl Harbor. With the 8 December Congressional Declaration of War on Japan, and the subsequent 11 December German and Italian Declaration of War on the United States, the U.S. became a full-fledged participant in the Second World War.

As a belligerent nation, the United States could no longer overlook the threat to the African air route posed by German operations from facilities under their control in Africa. U.S. officials believed that Bathurst, Gambia, was a security risk as it was situated less than 100 miles south of the Vichy French-held port and airfield in Dakar, Senegal. German military personnel were reportedly observed on the ground in Dakar. Furthermore, German reconnaissance aircraft had been active along the west coast of Africa.

The Allies deemed the security risk too high to continue to operate a main base in the Gambia. Liberia, an independent African state, with close historical ties to the United States, was selected as the next best location to serve as a western terminus for the trans-Africa air route. Thus, U.S. merchant

U.S. Air Corps Chief Major General Henry H. Arnold and his staff in a December 1941 planning session, looking over a globe of the world. (L to R) Lt. Col. Edgar P. Sorenson; Lt. Col. Harold L. George; Lt. Col. Arthur W. Vanaman; Major General Arnold; Major Edward S. Hansell, Jr.; Brig. Gen. Carl Spaats; Lt. Col. Arthur I. Ennis, Major Edward Scanlon. The Pan Am Boeing B-314 sits atop the globe in General Arnold's office. (National Archives)

ships loaded with construction gear for Pan Am operations, which were originally destined for Bathurst, were diverted to Liberia.

The route continued to evolve rapidly as the tide of battle changed in the Africa, Europe, and the China-Burma-India theaters of war. By April 1942, Pan Am-Africa had aircraft and air crews ranging out as far east as Kunming, China, and as far north as Kuybyshev, in the Soviet Union. Thus, PAA-Africa's mission had expanded greatly from the operational concept that was first developed in July 1941. PAA-Africa supported diverse wartime requirements, ranging from ferrying combat aircraft, to delivery of priority military equipment, carrying vital raw materials back to the United States, and evacuating military and civilian personnel from Burma.

PAA-Africa
Gears Up

As a result of his meetings in London and in Washington, Juan Trippe set out to plan and organize a modern air transport route that would cross Africa. The urgency of his mission was so critical to the British war effort that he began deploying people and equipment before implementation plans were completed and before formal contractual agreements were approved. Planners at Pan American Headquarters initially decided that at least 20 DC-3-type transport aircraft were required to conduct the in-Africa part of the mission. Additionally, prefabricated steel or concrete hotel facilities would be required to house personnel running the operation. Corporate Vice President H. M. Bixby directed that a survey team depart for Africa early in July 1941 to assess operational requirements, including living conditions, medical care, sanitary precautions, and other necessities needed for the operation in Africa. They were also charged to select the best location for establishing PAA-Africa's operations headquarters base in Africa. The team, which left New York on 4 July on a chartered flight, was directed to send its report back to New York via radio, to enable the company to begin immediate preparations, including the chartering of an ocean-going ship for the delivery of required heavy equipment and supplies.

Juan Trippe established two new operating subsidiaries to his existing Pan American Airways, Inc., to accomplish the projected contracts he was about to receive from the British and the United States Governments. The two new subsidiaries were, Pan American Airways-Africa, Limited (PAA-Africa) and Pan American Air Ferries, Inc. On 15 July 1941, the Pan American Airways System Headquarters, in the Chrysler Building in New York, issued System (Executive) Memorandum No. 58, which described the formation of the new corporation Pan American Airways-Africa, Ltd. The new subsidiary, a Delaware Corporation, was established as a temporary corporate identity. It was formed to provide air transport services between Bathurst, the Gambia, and Khartoum, Anglo-Egyptian Sudan, on a route that would pass through Takoradi and Accra in the Gold Coast, and Lagos, Nigeria. Other points would be added to the route as needed. The memorandum, signed by Juan

Frank Gledhill, later to become a vice-president of Pan American World Airways, was System Manager of PAA-Africa.

Trippe, was classified confidential and was addressed only to the Pan American Airways Executive Office, Staff Department Heads, and Division Managers. It also announced the upper echelon staff for the new company. The senior staff of PAA-Africa would include:

Franklin Gledhill	System Manager
George Kraigher	Operations Manager
John H. Yeomans	Assistant Manager
Karl Leuder	Assistant Operations Manager
Charles E. Shoemaker	Traffic Manager
James E. Weesner	Maintenance Superintendent
John Forbes	Field Auditor
R. R. Fife	Communications Superintendent
George Matrisciana	Senior Meteorologist
Dr. Chester Coggeshall	Senior Medical Officer
H. M. Bixby	Vice President of Pan American Airways, assigned duties as the Administrative Supervisor over all activities of PAA-Africa, Ltd.

Corporate records indicate that the original Directors of PAA-Africa, Ltd. were S. Sloan Colt, G. B. Grosvenor, E. O. McDonnell, Mark T. McKee, Thomas A. Morgan, J. T. Trippe and C. V. Whitney. Minutes of the initial corporate meetings of PAA-Africa Limited, show that the Directors were most concerned about the legal ramifications of their actions, under the provisions of the Neutrality Act, which had been amended in 1939.

Pan American Air Ferries Inc., the second new subsidiary formed, was incorporated on 23 July 1941, also in the State of Delaware. The principal job assigned to this new company was to ferry aircraft to allies of the United States in Africa, the Middle East, and eventually in the Soviet Union and other destinations.

Thus, Juan Trippe planned to use a total of three of his companies to accomplish the task presented to him by the British and United States Governments. Pan American Airways' Atlantic Division (one of several geographical Divisions in the corporate structure of the airline) would fly personnel and equipment from the United States to Brazil using DC-3 and other transport aircraft. These loads were then transferred to one of Pan American Atlantic Division's Boeing B-314 flying boats for the long flight across the South Atlantic. Upon arrival in Africa, a PAA-Africa DC-3-type aircraft would pick up the passengers and cargo from the Clippers and carry the loads across Africa to Cairo or other destinations. PAA-Air Ferries, Inc. provided Amer-

One of Pan American's Boeing 314s. These aircraft were vital to the United States effort to support the Allies in Europe during 1941–1942. B-314s made routine shuttle flights between Natal, Brazil, and Fisherman's Lake, Liberia. They were also used to support numerous "Special Missions," taking them to every corner of the globe.

ican pilots to ferry, under the provisions of the Lend-Lease Act, U.S.-manu-factured aircraft from the United States to Brazil, across the South Atlantic to the west coast of Africa, and then across Africa onward to various final desti-nations. The ferry pilots used the airports and other installations in Africa that were established and operated by PAA-Africa, Ltd.

In July 1941, Juan Trippe and his staff entered into formal negotia-tions with representatives of the British and United States Governments to formalize the arrangements that had been discussed in London and Wash-ington. By mid-August five new contracts were finalized and signed by the various parties. These included three contracts signed between PAA and its subsidiaries with the U.S. Government; and two contracts, one each signed by PAA-Africa, Ltd. and one by Pan American Air Ferries, Inc., with His Majesty's Government in the United Kingdom. The PAA-Africa Board of Directors formally approved the draft contracts, but not until their lawyers, Root, Clark, Buckner and Ballantine, approved the legality of the contracts under the Neutrality Act. Below are details of the these five contractual agreements:

CONTRACT #1
Contract No.: W 535 AC-21207.
Titled: Contract For Air Transport Service Between United States And West Africa, And For Equipment And Facilities In Connection Therewith.

Dated: August 12, 1941 (Amended on September 6, 1941)
Amount: $2,800,000.00
Signatories: U.S. War Department
          Pan American Airways, Company.

Provisions:
- Would provide for an air transport service between the United States and West Africa, establishing facilities in Miami, San Juan, Port of Spain, Belém and Natal, Brazil, and at least one point on the west coast of Africa.
- Pan American would operate an air transport service between Miami and the west coast of Africa.
- Passenger priority system would be controlled by the War Department.
- U.S. government to purchase Boeing Flying Boat No. NC-18612, (currently in service in the Pacific) and furnish it to PAA to use in this Atlantic service. Additionally, PAA to take two Sikorsky S-42B flying boats and deliver them to Manila to replace the Boeing.

- U.S. military aircraft were to have free rights to use all ground-based facilities established in support of this contract.
- U.S. government would pay PAA all costs and expenses.
- Contract would terminate 30 June 1942.

CONTRACT #2
Contract No.: DA-W535AC-415.
Titled: Contract For Air Transport Service Between African Points.
Dated: August 12, 1941 (Amended Dec. 13, 1941)
Amount: $7,613,945.00
Signatories: U.S. War Department
              Pan American Airways, Inc.
              Pan American Airways-Africa, Ltd.

Provisions:
- Provides for the organization of operation of an air transport service over the Trans-African Route between Bathurst, Teheran, and points in the U.S.S.R. via Khartoum and Basra and over a spur extending to Port Sudan.
- Includes the provision of all ground facilities, supplies and personnel.
- U.S. Government agrees to furnish 24 Douglas DC-3 aircraft to PAA-Africa.

CONTRACT #3
Contract No.: DA-W535AC-416
Titled: Contract For Ferrying Of Aircraft To African Points.
Dated: August 12, 1941 (Amended Dec. 13, 1941)
Amount: $10,186,055.00
Signatories: U.S. War Department
              Pan American Air Ferries, Inc.
              Pan American-Africa, Ltd.
              Pan American Airways, Inc.

Provisions:
- Provides for the ferrying of aircraft from Miami to the west coast of Africa by the Ferries Company. Then from the west coast of Africa, via Port Sudan and Basra to one or more points on the Trans-Africa or Singapore Routes.
- PAA-Africa, Ltd. will provide route services including gasoline, oil, maintenance, labor, and other supplies to Ferries at cost.
- Contract would terminate 30 June 1942.

CONTRACT #4
Contract No.: <u>No Number.</u>
Titled: No Title.
Dated: August 12, 1941
Amount: 30,000 pounds sterling
Signatories: His Majesty's Government in
        the United Kingdom (British Government)
        Pan American Airways-Africa, Ltd. (African)

Provisions:
The British Government agrees to:
- "Use its best endeavors to make arrangements with Anglo-Egyptian Sudan and all colonies, protectorates and mandated territories located on the Trans African Route for such permission as may be necessary to allow ... transport services to be initiated."
- Pay all taxes or duties imposed on African.
- Provide to African, without cost, "... the right to use ... all land, ground equipment, facilities and structures, including rest houses, now allocated to, and all additional land which may be required for the erection of new equipment, facilities, and structures, to be used in connection with, the Trans African Route."
- Give African control for safety purposes of the traffic at all airports on the route.
- Reserves the right to augment on a non-scheduled basis their use of their air transport service.
- Provide African with 30,000 pounds sterling to pay for wages of native labor.
- Retain overriding power to take control of all airports, radio, and other facilities on the Route in case of a military emergency.

CONTRACT #5
Contract No.: <u>No Number.</u>
Titled: No Title.
Dated: August 12, 1941
Amount: None stated.
Signatories: His Majesty's Government in
        the United Kingdom (British Government)
        Pan American Air Ferries, Inc. (Ferries)

Provisions:

The British Government agrees to:

- Make arrangements with Anglo-Egyptian Sudan and all colonies, protectorates, and mandated territories located on the Trans African Route for such permission as may be necessary to allow transport services to be initiated.
- Pay all taxes or duties imposed on Ferries.
- Provide to Ferries, without cost, the right to use all land, ground   equipment, facilities and structures, including rest houses in existence prior to the date of this agreement.
- Provide expeditious ingress and egress of all equipment, materials, supplies and personnel employed to support the American Ferry Agreement.
- Retain overriding power to take control of all airports, radio, and other facilities on the Route in case of a military emergency.

Each of these contractual agreements was classified SECRET by the U.S. Army. The corporate copies of the agreements were not marked as classified, but Pan American's Vice President, Bixby, did request that the Executive Office in New York keep the documents, "... in a locked file as the information contained therein is on the Army secret list."

In summary, Pan American agreed under contract to undertake the following tasks for the governments of Great Britain and the United States:

   1. Establish a scheduled transport service between the United States and West Africa.

   2. Construct an adequate airway across Africa, including the establishment of scheduled transport services and maintenance capabilities from West Africa to a terminal in Khartoum. (Later extended further east.)

   3. Organize and operate an aircraft ferry service to deliver Lend-Lease aircraft from the United States to a point in the Middle East or Russia.

The project had the total support of the United States Government. The government provided the capital, ensured that the highest priorities were assigned to PAA-Africa's shipping requirements and acquisition of materials, and supplied the aircraft that PAA-Africa would use to operate the transport service in Africa.

At 1700 on 18 August 1941, the White House issued the following statement that was subsequently published in many of the nation's leading newspapers:

The President announced today an important step to speed delivery of planes direct to the British forces in the Middle East. Agreements have been concluded under which the Pan American Airways System will ferry aircraft from the United States to West Africa and then will ferry those planes on to the Middle East. In connection with the ferry system, Pan American Airways is establishing an air transport service from West Africa to the Middle East and plans are under way for a transport service from the United States to West Africa. Planes owned by the United States Government will be used by Pan American and they will be operated by American personnel. The route of delivery is so arranged that it will nowhere pass through the zone of actual warfare. The transport service will supplement the ferry service by returning ferry personnel and carrying spare plane parts and items essential to effective delivery of aircraft to the Middle East. This route will also be available for general commercial use, providing direct air service from New York or Baltimore to Africa. The ferry system and the transport service provide direct and speedy delivery of aircraft from "the arsenal of Democracy" to a critical point in the front against aggression. The importance of this direct line of communication between our country and strategic out posts in Africa cannot be over-estimated.

Although this proclamation placed American civilians in the combat zone, there was little public comment or debate about the President's actions. Ominous war news from Europe and news reel coverage of the recently concluded "Atlantic Charter" discussions with Prime Minister Churchill effectively distracted any opposition to President Roosevelt's proclamation.

On 19 August 1941, the Board of PAA-Africa, Ltd. gave Full Power of Attorney rights to John H. Yeomans. As the Assistant Manager for all aspects of PAA-Africa, Ltd., he was designated as the company's official representative in Africa and was given the right to act for the company in Liberia, Portuguese Guinea, The Gambia, Anglo-Egyptian Sudan, Sierra Leone, Gold Coast, and Nigeria.

The next big step was to locate enough men to build and operate the route. Pan American Airways' recruiting office put out the call for pilots, carpenters, mechanics, cooks, construction workers, clerical staff, finance officers, doctors, and nurses.

Advertisements were placed in most of the major newspapers in the nation. Bill Kent, who responded to an advertisement he saw in a newspaper in San Diego, California, was hired to serve as a maintenance superintendent in the aircraft dispersal area in Accra.

Pan American Airways' geographical Divisions were asked to give up key employees so that they could work for the new PAA-Africa subsidiary. For example, Voit Gilmore moved from the Eastern Division to be the Personnel Director of PAA-Africa on the orders of Mr. Trippe. Others who had returned from the Pacific Division, after the Japanese attack on Pearl Harbor, were reassigned from Pan American's Pacific Division to PAA-Africa.

Senior executives went on extended recruiting trips to locate personnel. Pan Am President Juan Trippe used his network of fellow students from Yale's Class of 1921 to locate classmates, and sons of classmates, who agreed to sign-on with PAA-Africa. Even Juan Trippe's office boy, Parker (Peter) Wiseman, signed up after he saw a notice on the bulletin board at the Pan Am offices in the Chrysler Building in New York.

Civilian aviation schools, that were teaching young men how to become aircraft mechanics and radio operators, were also considered to be prime targets for the PAA-Africa recruiters. Schools included the Atlantic Aviation Co. in Delaware; the Rising Sun School of Aeronautics in Philadelphia, Pennsylvania; the Northeast Aviation School in Boston, Mass., and Burlington, Vermont; the J.M. Perry Institute in Yakima, Washington; the Apprentice Training School in Syracuse, New York; the Melville Aeronautical Radio School in New York; and

Future PAA-Africa pilots Art Dorman, Don Swanson, Ed Frankiewicz, and their flight instructor Len Eagles at the Civilian Pilot Training Course at Bridgeport, Connecticut, in the summer of 1941. They look very young—and they were.

Page Aviation, Rochester, New York. Recruiters convinced some students to leave their training early with the promises of follow-on training in Africa.

Recruiters were particularly interested in any applicant who had completed the Civil Pilot Training Program (CPTP) or had a "ham" radio license. The recruiters would arrive at the schools and tell the prospective applicants that they were authorized by President Roosevelt and Juan Trippe to ask for volunteers to go to Africa to pioneer a flight route through Africa. Who could resist such an opportunity? [See Appendix A for a copy of a recruiting letter from a Pan American Airways representative.]

Despite the flurry of recruiting activity there was still a shortage of qualified pilots. The War Department agreed initially to release 40 pilots from active duty assignments so that they could fly with PAA-Africa. To facilitate the process, Pan American recruiters and senior Army officers went directly to the Army's flight training bases and actively recruited Army officers to volunteer to leave the U.S. Army and become pilots for PAA-Africa.

At Gunter Field in Alabama, ten newly assigned 2nd Lt. Instructor Pilots were recruited by an Army Colonel from Washington. He told the pilots that he needed volunteers to fly as co-pilots with PAA-Africa, Ltd. He briefed the young aviators that they would be placed on Inactive Reserve Status with the U.S. Army, fly as co-pilots for PAA-Africa, Ltd., and be credited for active duty time, as approved in writing, by the Secretary of War.

More than 1,000 men were hired by PAA-Africa. Each of the new hires received the following issued gear:

6 pairs of trousers	1 tropical helmet
2 khaki coats	12 shirts
1 rain coat	

Each man also needed briefings, inoculations, medical checks, letters to draft boards, and passports before they could depart for Africa. Pan American's Vice President in charge of the Washington office, Anne Archibald, played a major role in obtaining passports and official clearances for the men to travel to Africa.

By early September 1941 it became obvious that the company was still going to be short of pilots. Of several possible options for obtaining additional pilots, the company posited that the U.S. Army Air Corps was the preferred source. In a 17 September memorandum to Major General H. H. Arnold, Chief of Combat Air Forces, the company laid out their rationale for having the Army release another 80 pilots in addition to the 40 pilots that had already been agreed to:

...We believe this is the desirable alternative from the Government's point of view and would result in the following mutual advantages to the Army and PAA:

(a) Training of Army pilots in civil transport procedure.

(b) Familiarization of Army pilots with meteorological, navigational and other operating problems in Africa and the consequent obtaining of information valuable to the military service of the United States;

(c) Conduct of the Trans-African ferry and transport services in an efficient and disciplined manner—which will otherwise be next to impossible without raiding either the British or the Domestics (airlines) or both.

Eventually, additional Army pilots were released to fly with PAA-Africa. On 2 October 1941, the following Western Union Telegram was sent to Kelly Field, Texas, where recruiters were also active:

CONFIRMING TELEPHONE INSTRUCTIONS TO ADJU-TANT KELLY FIELD TODAY OKAY FOR ELEVEN OFFIC-ERS REPORT TO 4406 CHRYSLER BLDG NEW YORK MONDAY MORNING OCTOBER THIRTEENTH AT NINE O'CLOCK. HAVE ALL OFFICERS GET NEW PASSPORT PICTURES MADE TODAY IN CIVILIAN CLOTHES AND FORWARD SIX PRINTS AIR MAIL SPECIAL TO MRS. A. M. ARCHIBALD PAN AMERICAN AIRWAYS SYSTEM BO-WEN BLDG 815 5TH STREET ROOM 638 WASHINGTON DC TONIGHT WITHOUT FAIL.
-= PAN AMERICAN AIRWAYS AFRICA KRISTOFFERSON.

In addition to initial pilot training bases, PAA-Africa's recruiters visited some of the Army's operational flying units. John T. "Pat" Passage was flying B-17s at MacDill Field in Tampa, Florida, when PAA's Senior Pilot Henry C. Kristofferson visited the field and recruited Pat and several other pilots out of the Army Air Corps.

Pilot contracts provided for a basic salary of $755.00 per month for Captains and $350.00 per month for Co-Pilots while they were assigned to foreign duty. [See Appendix B for a sample signed PAA-Africa, Ltd. employment contract.]

After the initial cadre of pilots was selected and sent to Africa, PAA realized that they would need to establish a training center to ensure that

*Pan American Air
Ferries School
building in Miami,
previously operated as
the Terrace Club.*

replacements would be available when needed. Pan American Air Ferries, Inc. was assigned the responsibilities of establishing and operating the Pan Am pilot training school on the grounds of the old Terrace Club on 119th St. NW in Miami.

The first Commander/Director of the school was Captain C. W. Dewey. The training program for junior pilots lasted almost six months and consisted of the following major areas of instruction:
- Instrument flight
- Meteorology
- Power Plant
- Radio code (required a minimum transmitting and receiving speed
   of thirteen words per minute to pass.)
- Navigation
   — Dead reckoning
   — Radio navigation
   — Celestial navigation.

These were considered the most basic principles of flight operations, that every new PAA-Africa pilot needed to understand before he could be assigned to flight duties in Africa. The first class, consisting of 32 pilots, graduated from the school as Class 42-A on 24 April 1942.

(Top) Graduate Harry Bernard speaking from the Head Table during Graduation ceremony for PAA Air Ferries School, Class 42-A, April 1942, while Pan Am President Juan Trippe (on his left) seems to approve.
(Bottom) Graduation Certificate awarded to Edward Frankiewicz for completing the Pan American Air Ferries School's Junior Pilots Course.

Another serious hurdle facing PAA-Africa, as it geared up for the Africa operation, was the lack of standardization with the aircraft equipment provided by the U.S. Government. Article III, Sub-section (1) of the basic contract #DA-W535AC-415, stated that:

> ...it being understood that all aircraft so to be furnished to African (term used in contract text for PAA-Africa) shall be a substantially uniform type of power plant and uniform types of other equipment...

Most of the aircraft the government obtained and gave to PAA-Africa had to be held in the United States to be updated and modified to meet basic company standards. For example, in early November 1941, numerous aircraft had to be held in depots for modification work because of their non-standard engines and internal configurations. Six DC-3s and DC-2s that were in Miami, designated for service in Africa, had a total of five different types of engines installed. Parts inventories in Africa were established to support only two types of engines: the Wright G-102A and the P&W 1830. Additionally, some of the aircraft were configured as sleepers, club sleepers, and as standard commercial passenger transports which severely limited their usefulness for the mission in Africa.

With signed contracts in hand, Juan Trippe and his PAA-Africa, Ltd. were ready to undertake what many considered to be the largest single transport assignment heretofore undertaken by a civilian airline. Time was now running out for the British forces in North Africa. The real question was: could PAA-Africa do the job of organizing, building, operating, and maintaining the trans-Africa air route in time to influence the outcome of the battles then being fought in the desert of North Africa?

Hustling East

*Now it is not good for the Christian's health to hustle the Aryan
brown,
For the Christian riles, and the Aryan smiles, and it weareth the
Christian down;
And the end of the fight, is a tombstone white, with the name of
the late deceased,
And the epitaph drear, "A fool lies here, who tried to hustle the
East."*

— *Rudyard Kipling*

By August 1941 Pan American-Africa, Limited had already started to disprove Kipling's earlier admonition that, "A fool lies here, who tried to hustle the East." Pan Am's senior staff had begun to move men and gear eastward several weeks before the contractual agreements were signed on 12 August 1941. In July Pan Am V.P., and now PAA-Africa's System Manager Franklin Gledhill and his Assistant Operations Manager Karl Leuder flew to Bathurst, Gambia, on board a special mission B-314 Clipper piloted by Captain Harold Gray, to take a first-hand look at the proposed route. The two men proceeded to Takoradi, Gold Coast, on a DC-2 where they met Vernon Crudge, the British Overseas Airways Corporation's Director for Africa. Crudge, who was based in Nairobi, was instructed to meet Gledhill and assist him in his survey mission. Crudge played a vital role, as he was able to introduce Gledhill to all the British Governors, Generals, and Colonial Secretaries, etc. assigned to the region. He also offered the use of his de Havilland 86 biplane to survey the entire air route. Gledhill had been trained as a mining engineer and made detailed decisions about equipment needed to bring the austere air route up to modern-day specifications. The small group moved quickly across Africa; they were in Kano on the 8th of August, Khartoum on the 11th, Cairo on the 13th, and Asmara on the 16th. Gledhill and Crudge became close friends during this mission and this helped to ensure a good working relationship between their two airline companies as the new PAA-Africa began to operate in Africa.

Gledhill returned to New York by the end of August, but Karl Leuder remained in Africa to lay additional groundwork for the operation. On 2 September, Leuder left Monrovia, Liberia, by open surf boat for Fisherman's Lake, located on Liberia's coastal region near the border with Sierra Leone. His mission was to assess the possibility of using this lake as a flying boat base for Pan Am's large Boeing B-314 Clippers.

The First Wave

In New York, Gledhill began the personnel and equipment deployment phase of this operation by ensuring that 36 seats were available to his staff on the Pan Am Clipper, scheduled to leave New York's LaGuardia Marine Terminal on Wednesday, 24 September 1941. Gledhill wrote that,

> This transportation is required in order to get executive personnel from the various departments, along with pilots and mechanics, to Africa approximately three weeks in advance of arrival of the steamline shipment with the bulk of the personnel aboard. We believe that not less than three weeks will be required in order that the personnel concerned may make the proper arrangements for 250 personnel arriving in Africa in the middle of October, along with the equipment for our main base at Accra.

Seat quotas were established on the B-314 flight so each of PAA-Africa's major operating departments could send their initial permanent-party staff members to Africa. The quotas were: Executive–1, Operations–16, Maintenance–13, Construction–1, Traffic–1, Communications–1, Accounting–1, Medical–1, and Commissary–1.

Frank Gledhill also directed that the initial PAA-Africa, aircraft fleet, consisting of six DC-3s ferried to Africa, should be in place when the B-314 arrived in Bathurst, Gambia. These aircraft were fitted with internally-mounted additional fuel tanks to enable them to make the long jouney to Africa. He also directed that the crews ferrying the aircraft should be prepared to return to the United States on the B-314.

The first Pan Am Clipper flight, carrying PAA-Africa's staff to Africa, departed from the Marine Terminal at LaGuardia Field in New York at 1420 on 27 September 1941.

The plan was for this first group of select staff to fly to Bathurst on board the B-314 Clipper and then transfer to PAA-Africa's DC-3s for the

*(L to R) Jim Weesner (Maintenance Supervisor), Bill Wersen (Junior Engineer),
Harry Driver (Shop Superintendent), and Johnnie Newman (Maintenance
Secretary) dressed informally, as was the custom at that time; preparing to board*
Clipper Cape Town *in New York, bound for Africa, 27 September 1941.*

flight to Accra, Gold Coast. En route to Bathurst the Clipper made stops in
Bermuda, Trinidad, Belém, and Natal.

On 1 October 1941, 39 PAA-Africa, Ltd. employees arrived in Accra,
Gold Coast and PAA-Africa, Ltd. began its African odyssey.

*PAA Boeing-314, the
Cape Town Clipper,
is serviced at
LaGuardia before its
27 September 1941
departure for Africa.*

Early arrivals in Accra, in October 1941. This photograph shows Frank Pierlas and Pop Feaster (top and center) and one of the first DC-3s to arrive in Africa.

The Second Wave

The second group of men destined for West Africa departed from Pier 18, North River, New York, at 2115, on 9 October aboard the *S.S. Acadia*, of the Barber Steamship Line. The manifest included 195 men and a large quantity of heavy equipment. The men were members of the Maintenance, Communications, Operations, Medical, Traffic, Executive, Commissary, and Construction Departments of PAA-Africa. They were sworn to secrecy concerning their destination and their travel schedule because of German U-Boat activity in the Atlantic. There was considerable consternation at the pier when they

Passengers getting some sun on the deck of the S.S. Acadia.
Note the hatch covers painted with the American flag to show Axis airmen that this ship was a non-belligerent in October, 1941.

heard that the *New York Daily News* carried headlines and a detailed story about PAA-Africa's mission on the day of their departure.

During a stop in Port of Spain, the ship's crew discovered aviation fuel stored with the other cargo and went on strike for higher pay because of the perceived additional dangers inherent with transporting the fuel. Once the issue was resolved, the ship continued on its way down the east coast of South America and crossed the Equator on 19 October with a three-ship U.S. Navy escort. The journey proceeded routinely until they reached Recife, Brazil. The ship's Skipper, Captain Allen, briefed Dr. G. M. Saunders, the senior Pan Am representative, that the U.S. Navy escort ships would not proceed eastward with them past the 36th meridian. At that point, the Captain explained, the *Acadia* would become part of a British convoy heading east across the South Atlantic. Dr. Saunders protested against this plan, arguing that an American civilian vessel should not join a British convoy of combatant vessels. His protest was passed to Washington, and a reply was received, ordering the U.S. Navy ships to escort the *Acadia* all the way to Africa. During the remainder of the voyage, the standard "zig-zag" pattern was used and many of the passengers slept on deck at night with their life jackets on, for fear of German U-Boat attacks.

Living conditions on board the *Acadia* were less than pleasant during the voyage from Trinidad to Takoradi. PAA employees were assigned to some of the least desirable cabins. Accommodations consisted of three men assigned to rooms with only two bunks, no sheets or blankets, insufficient ventilation, and no fresh water showers.

Upon reaching Africa, the *Acadia* first docked in Lagos, Nigeria, on 28 October 1941. The passengers had to spend five days on board the vessel, while 450 tons of PAA-Africa cargo was off-loaded in Lagos. This included 15 electric refrigerators, one electric ice cream freezer, numerous power lawn mowers, phonographic records, one radio, 15 tons of condensed milk, and 3,000 cases of beer. Because *Acadia* was a passenger vessel, cargo loading and unloading was extremely slow as it had to pass through side ports. The vessel also loaded on some cargo destined for the United States and subsequently sailed westward and docked in Takoradi, Gold Coast. The PAA-Africa employees finally disembarked from the *Acadia* on 4 November 1941. From the port, some of the personnel boarded PAA-Africa aircraft while others boarded buses for the final 100-mile leg of their journey to Accra. (It was later learned that the British convoy, in which the *Acadia* was supposed to be on the South Atlantic crossing, had been attacked by German submarines and the ships scattered.)

The Third Wave

The next major movement of men and equipment left New York on the motor ship *East Indian* on 23 November 1941. It carried 300 men, most of them construction personnel, and more than 10,500 tons of prefabricated housing, which had been ordered through Clinton Bush for PAA-Africa. This was the last ship scheduled to use the port at Bathurst. After the bombing of Pearl Harbor, Bathurst was declared unsafe because its location was too close to Vichy French territory. When it arrived at Bathurst on 8 December 1941, the *East Indian* was directed not to discharge its cargo, but to take it to Liberia. The ship arrived off the coast of Liberia late in December near Fisherman's Lake, where it was off-loaded through the surf by native long boats. Thus, Liberia became the newly-designated western terminus to the rapidly-developing trans-Africa air route.

The next ship to depart for Africa was the *S.S. Santa Paula*, of the Grace Lines. It left New York City, under the command of Captain Walter N. Prengel, on 3 December 1941. The Atlantic crossing for this speedy ship was relatively routine, except for one close encounter with a German U-Boat. Passenger Bernard Sherwood recalls the event vividly: While on deck one evening Bernie noticed a huge black object just a few yards to the starboard side of the *Santa Paula*. A moment later he could see that it was a German submarine, apparently running on the surface to recharge its batteries, with most of its crew on deck enjoying fresh air and some night-time physical exercise. He quickly notified the bridge and as the German submarine sounded its crash-dive klaxon, the *Santa Paula* went to full speed, and was able to out-run the now submerged U-Boat. The news of the air attack on Pearl Harbor reached the ship when it was halfway across the Atlantic. During the rest of the voyage it followed standard evasive techniques and sailed a zig-zag course. The remainder of the voyage was uneventful. As they approached the coast of Africa, British four-engined Sunderland patrol bombers met them and provided an air escort to the Gambia.

The ship made an unscheduled stop in the harbor at Bathurst for a quick paint job before continuing its journey. The crew and passengers all chipped in to paint the entire ship gray with some camouflage. While at anchor in the mouth of the Gambia River, the crew and passengers watched as a German reconnaissance aircraft, flying out of Dakar, Senegal, made daily passes over the area.

The *Santa Paula* also made a port call at Freetown, in Sierra Leone. They were trapped in the port for days by the arrival of a huge British convoy of merchant ships. For more than 24 hours, the convoy came into the harbor, one ship at a time, effectively blocking the *Santa Paula* in the port. Freetown was home to a major British naval refueling depot and the harbor was well protected by mines and a submarine gate made out of wire mesh. The *Santa Paula* eventually made it out of the harbor to its final destination, Takoradi, in the Gold Coast. There, the passengers and cargo were unloaded, the trucks first, and then the rest of PAA-Africa's cargo onto the trucks for the drive to Accra. Crated Lend-Lease P-40 aircraft were off-loaded and taken to the British airfield at Takoradi for reassembly.

Pan American's Boeing B-314 Clippers, loaded with PAA-Africa personnel and some cargo, were now making routine shuttle flights between Brazil and the west coast of Africa. While the flights may have been routine, not all of them left without a hitch. Early in December 1941, one group of PAA-Africa passengers actually began their journey to Africa by train. Bad weather had delayed the arrival of a Clipper in to New York, so the passengers were instructed to take a train to Miami so as to meet an aircraft bound for San Juan, Puerto Rico. By the time the train reached Charleston, South Carolina, the weather cleared. Plans were again quickly changed and the PAA-Africa passengers were taken off the train in Charleston and placed on a Pan

Group of PAA-Africans boarding a Pan American B-307 leaving Charleston, South Carolina, en route to Africa on 5 December 1941. Included in this photo are (top to bottom of stairs) #2-Don J. Stoeger, #7-Dallas B. Sherman, #8-John T. Passage, #9-James H. Hubbard, #11-Charles R. Heffner, #12-Stuart H. Murphy, #15-Ivan W. (Wayne) Eveland, and 16-Henry C. Kristofferson.

Am Boeing 307 aircraft for the flight to San Juan, where they finally boarded the Pan Am Clipper for the flight across the South Atlantic to Africa.

While most of the South Atlantic crossings accomplished by aircraft were uneventful, the air crews were always on the lookout for German U-Boats and suspicious looking "tramp steamers." There were occasions when these German surface ships would fire on low flying aircraft as they passed overhead.

By early December 1941, large quantities of heavy and bulky equipment were arriving in Africa. Their cargoes included vehicles, such as Ford tank trucks, G.M.C. truck trailer units, Fruehauf trailers, Chevrolet carryalls, and their spare parts, such as drive shafts, rear springs, filters, headlights, and transmissions. These were transported on ships whose names included: *Zarembo*, *Balby*, *West Kebar*, *West Irmo*, and the *S.S. Otho*. Not all of these vessels completed their voyages. German U-Boats were very active off the West African coast and several of the ships carrying Pan American cargo never made it to their destinations. Records indicate that by December 1942, more than 15,521 weight tons or 38,802 measurement tons (40 cubic feet each) of supplies had been shipped to West African and Red Sea ports, destined for the initial 18 installations manned by Pan American Airways-Africa. Large cargo items for PAA-Africa's main operating base in Accra were shipped by sea through Takoradi. Large cargo shipments for Kano and Maiduguri in Nigeria were unloaded at the port in Lagos and trans-shipped via rail and/or road to these sites. Bulky cargo for Khartoum, El Fasher, and El Geneina was unloaded at Port Sudan on the Red Sea, then trans-shipped by rail to Khartoum and El Obeid, then via truck or camel across desert paths to the sites in western Sudan. As the scope of the flight operations expanded, more U.S. merchant vessels sailed for Africa.

On 15 February 1942, the *S.S. Fairfax* left New York for West Africa. This vessel, originally of the Merchant and Minors Transportation Company, but now part of the Atlantic, Gulf, and West Indies Steamship Lines, was operated under contract to the War Shipping Administration as a Special War Department Mission. The *Fairfax* was armed with a 4-inch gun, a 3-inch-high angle anti-aircraft gun, two .50-caliber and two .30-caliber anti-aircraft machine guns.

The *Fairfax* carried a variety of passengers, including PAA-Africa employees, Firestone employees of the American-owned rubber plantation in Liberia, and U.S Army officers and enlisted men en route to several different duty stations located in Africa and the Middle East. Of the total of 395 passengers, 60 PAA employees were manifested on this voyage to Lagos, Nigeria. The trip took 33 days. The ship was slow (only 13 knots) and the food and

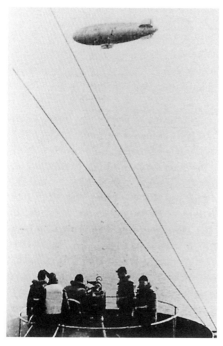

The S.S. Fairfax under way to Africa with the U.S. Navy's K-6 blimp escort.

living conditions on board were considered by all to be awful. The ship was quickly rechristened the *S.S. Pig's Knuckles* by its hungry passengers, and it experienced many problems en route as the skipper and his crew were not really qualified for this, their first open ocean voyage. On one occasion, after experiencing an on-board epidemic of flu-like illnesses, the Senior U.S. Army officer on board, on the advice of his senior surgeon, posted armed guards in the ship's galley to make sure that the ship's stewards used more sanitary methods in preparing the food, including washing the dishes between sittings.

On 19 March 1942, the *S.S. Frederick Lykes* sailed from Pier 10 on Staten Island for a 15,000-nautical-mile journey to Africa. Sixteen PAA employees were on board, along with a full load of wartime cargo. They included: Leslie Cottrell, Joe Dunn, J. F. Flannery, Ed Murphy, E. J. Ryan, R. J. Tirado, Dennis Williams, H. Whitehead, T. H. Phillips, Smith, Charles Murphy, Charles Wilson, R. J. James, Pete Hughes, Howard Jensen, and Bob Morrow. The *Frederick Lykes* was a C3 type freighter constructed in 1941 and was relatively fast. It was armed with a 5.50" gun aft, a 3.30" gun forward, and with several .50-caliber machine guns. PAA employees were pressed into service to stand four-hour deck watches and to serve as powder and projectile loaders on the ship's heavier weapons and machine gunners. Gun and lifeboat drills were frequent during the entire voyage. Fortunately, no shots were fired in anger.

The *Frederick Lykes* was escorted by an assortment of military aircraft, blimps, and U.S. Naval surface vessels as it sailed south along the east coast of the United States. The escort was necessary because of the increased risk from German submarines operating off the coast. The passengers witnessed

Bob Morrow standing watch on the deck of the S.S. Frederick Lykes *during his long crossing to Africa. After arriving at Port Sudan, He and 15 other PAA personnel were then flown to Accra, Gold Coast.*

the remains of many sunken ships with only their funnels and superstructures showing above water. The escorts terminated their security coverage when the *Frederick Lykes* sailed past the Caribbean region. Thereafter, she sailed alone

After 27 days at sea, the *Frederick Lykes* pulled into Cape Town, South Africa. With only one day of shore leave the passengers had little time to do much more than get off the boat and stretch their sea legs. The ship then departed for her final destination, Port Sudan, which was the Anglo-Egyptian Sudan's only modern sea port on the Red Sea. The trip from New York to Port Sudan took 42 days. But, for the PAA men the 15,000-mile trip was not over when they walked off the ship at Port Sudan. They were loaded on to PAA-Africa's C-47s and flown a further 3,000 miles back across Africa to Accra.

Some PAA-Africans relaxing on the deck of the S.S. Frederick Lykes *during the voyage to Africa.*

PAA-Africa, Ltd., deployed more than 2,000 personnel to Africa for the operation of the air route. Only two employees were known to have been lost during transit; both men drowned in the sinking of the *S.S. Otho* by enemy action.

Welcome to Africa

When the first group arrived in Accra early in October, they found living conditions to be less than adequate: no running water, no electricity, and food that was classified by most of the men as "lousy." Most of the new facilities, ordered by Gledhill and Leuder during their visit in July, were still being constructed by the British contractors.

Some of the first men to reach Accra had to be redeployed immediately to their final destinations at the various stations located along the route. Those hired to perform duties as Operations Officers were part of this group that needed to be redeployed. Because all of these individuals were college-educated, and for the most part had no aviation management experience, the personnel department's decision-making process was somewhat informal. Their assignments were determined by lottery.

The Herculean task of organizing all of these shipments to Africa fell to Daniel G. Vucetich and his staff of two, operating out of a 9' x 12' office on the 44th floor of the Chrysler Building in New York City. The list of items procured by this office and shipped to Africa is long and inclusive. In an internal Pan Am document, Vucetich listed the items that he and his staff shipped to Africa. These comprised:

> 400 cases of refrigerators, 500 cases of radio equipment, such as transmitters, transformers and the parts thereof; upwards of 1,000,000 board feet of lumber, finished and rough, among which we had some ply-wood, 3,750 cases of beer, pepsi-cola, coca-cola, and soda water. 5,000 bundles of structural steel for the hangars, power houses, etc., 10 tractors, 4 road scrapers, 500 cases of automobile parts, 1,500 cases of airplane parts, 15,000 bags of cement, 20 station wagons; 20 sedans, 25 trucks; 15 buses; 15 tank-trucks; 24 prefabricated houses, each weighing 88,000 lbs.; 500 barrels of assorted sizes of nails; finished nails, galvanized nails and spikes, 500 ash cans, and a half-dozen boxes of Christmas presents for the boys on the front; about 2,000 bundles of conduit for electrical equipment, 50 cases of telephone equipment, 50 Lorrimer Diesel engines which came from Oakland,

International Harvester promoting its products that were used by PAA-Africa in the early stages of building up the Trans-Africa Air Route.

Calif., each weighing 10,000 lbs.; 12 crash trucks; 20 army trucks; 750 reels of copper cable; each reel weighing about 3,000 lbs; 200 reels of steel cable, each reel weighting about 3,500 lbs; 500 hand trucks; 35 electric baggage trucks, which are run with a little motor, and about 750 drums of paint.

Corporate records show that 15,521 weight tons had been shipped to Africa by 2 December 1943. This equated to 38,802.5 measurement tons (a measurement ton is equal to 40 cubic feet and is used as an indicator of the bulkiness of the cargo). Most of these items were procured and shipped with little fanfare. PAA employees had been briefed on the "secret" nature of their mission and great care was taken to keep this information out of the public domain. There were, however, several notable exceptions as exemplified by the two advertisements illustrated.

On 23 October 1941, with only the initial cadre of men and equipment established in place along the route, the first scheduled flight of a PAA-Africa, Ltd. aircraft had taken off from Accra to Khartoum. The initial schedule had

*Pan American Airways
System telling its own story
in a November 1941
advertisement in the Pan Am
Magazine,* New Horizons.

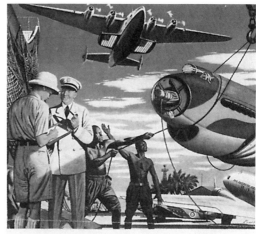

AMERICA'S NEW LIFELINE TO AFRICA

PAN AMERICAN AIRWAYS SYSTEM

been three round trips per week, but this schedule changed radically after the
bombing of Pearl Harbor and the United States declared war. PAA-Africa
would henceforth modify its flight operations frequently to provide support to
the ever-changing wartime requirements levied upon it by the United States
and British Governments.

Operating Locations for PAA-Africa

PAA-Africa established and operated flight support installations for the African resupply route under the terms of the 1941 contract with the British and American Governments.

... between Bathurst, Gambia, and Khartoum, Egypt, with intermediate stops at Freetown, Monrovia, Takoradi, Accra, Lagos, Kano, Maiduguri, El Fasher and El Obeid, or between other terminal points and/or with such other intermediate stops as may be mutually agreed upon by the parties hereto.

Initially, 18 stations were manned by PAA-Africa personnel. These were eventually expanded to include additional airfields in the Middle East, the Persian Gulf, the Arabian Peninsula, and as far east as Calcutta, India.

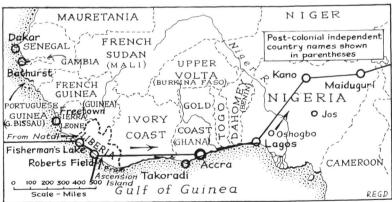

This map shows the main PAA Africa bases in West Africa. Headquarters of the organization was at Accra, in the British Gold Coast colony, now Ghana. Trans-Atlantic landfall was, for the flying boats, Fisherman's Lake, and for the landplanes, Roberts Field, in Liberia.

Bathurst, Gambia

Bathurst was a logical site to serve as the initial western terminus to the trans-Africa route. As a British colony, it was well situated geographically for both the sea-based Boeing B-314 Clippers of Pan American Airways and the land-based cargo aircraft operated by PAA-Africa. The flying boat mooring was in the wide mouth of the Gambia River. The first of several groups of PAA-Africa employees landed in Bathurst on board the B-314 Clippers. Personnel were then transferred to PAA-Africa's transport aircraft for the next leg of their journey to Accra, in the Gold Coast.

The first flight of a PAA-Africa aircraft in Africa is credited to Captain Frank Glen at Bathurst on 1 October, 1941.

After 7 December 1941, there was serious concern about security in Bathurst, because of the proximity of two Axis-controlled and -fortified ports. Dakar, Senegal, was located 100 miles to the north and Abidjan, Ivory Coast, 900 miles to the southeast. Because of this concern, the western terminus of the route was moved from the Gambia to Liberia. Construction plans and the scheduling of the B-314 Clippers through Bathurst were suspended. Nonetheless, PAA-Africa continued to operate scheduled cargo service from Accra to Bathurst until 12 June 1942.

Freetown, Sierra Leone

By 1941, Freetown, Sierra Leone, situated some 422 miles southeast of Bathurst, was already a major British wartime naval base. British ship convoys would stop at Free-town for refueling, repairs, and for refuge from the German U-Boat threat in the South Atlantic. The airport at Freetown was used by an

The first PAA personnel to arrive in Bathurst in September 1941.

R.A.F. detachment and a small group of PAA-Africa staff. The R.A.F. protected the large British convoys of surface ships which were calling at Freetown. PAA-Africa manned a station at the airport from December 1941 through 15 September 1942. At the height of operations 15 PAA-Africa employees were stationed there.

The amenities in Freetown were austere. Water was transported to the airfield by truck until June 1942 , when a well was dug. Two staff houses were constructed eventually with water closets and septic systems.

Liberia

Liberia, an independent republic, was one of only four countries on the African continent that had an established American Legation, with official U.S. Government representatives. As an independent African state, Liberia presented some interesting opportunities but some serious logistic and

political problems for PAA-Africa's planners. They were not constrained there by having to work solely through representatives of the British government. But this was a mixed blessing, as they had to work closely with both the U.S. Department of State and the Liberian Government to obtain operating approvals.

Mr. Hibbard, U.S. Chargé d'Affaires, leaves the American Legation building in Monrovia. May 1942. (National Archives)

Pan American's headquarters also found that it could not rely on the existence of a British-established rudimentary infrastructure, on which they could build their operation. But Pan Am did have the benefit of working with an independent African government that was quite friendly to the American cause. PAA-Africa was also able to use many amenities already in place at the large rubber plantation owned and operated by the American industrialist Harvey Firestone. The Firestone Plantation Company, a large raw rubber producing operation, was centered near the city of Harbel.

Pan American Airways, Inc. and PAA-Africa, Ltd. worked together, first to establish, then to operate, three aircraft landing fields in Liberia. These were: Fisherman's Lake seaplane base, the adjacent Benson Field landplane airfield, and Roberts Field, a large landplane airfield located near Harbel, adjacent to the Firestone Plantation.

Fisherman's Lake

In the search for a seaplane base for the Boeing B-314 Clippers, Pan American conducted several surveys of the West Africa coastline. Lake Piso, located in western Liberia, just inland from the Atlantic coastline, near the

Typical street scene in Monrovia, the capital of Liberia. June 1942. (National Archives)

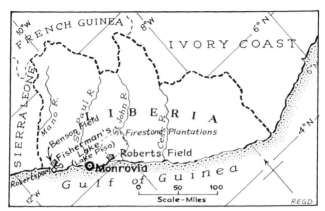

Pan American Airways established PAA-Africa several months before the United States entered the Second World War. Liberia, an independent nation, was a convenient and attractive first destination for aircraft crossing the Atlantic Ocean. Lake Piso, renamed Fisherman's Lake, became the flying boat base, while Roberts Field was built on the edge of the Firestone rubber plantation. Benson Field was also constructed on the lakeside, using P.S.P. (Perforated Steel Plate) imported by ship at the nearby port.

border with Sierra Leone, was first surveyed from the air by Captain Harold Gray in July 1941. Gray examined several sites and confirmed it as the preferred operating location, subsequently renamed Fisherman's Lake or just "Fish Lake." Pan Am's staff had hoped for a site much closer to the Firestone Plantation, but there were no sites for flying boats in that region.

No Walking On Water
While Captain Gray was conducting his aerial survey of landing sites in Liberia, he was giving serious consideration to a site near the city of Monrovia. There is a river and lagoon system near the town and if it could be used as a landing site it would have been much closer to the Firestone Plantation than the site at Fisherman's Lake. From the air, the body of water looked as if it was large enough for flying boat operations, but was it deep enough? Gray made a low pass over the water to try to make a final determination. During a second low pass he flew directly over a native fishing from a small boat. As the aircraft passed overhead, the fisherman jumped out of his boat and ran towards the shore. Gray had his answer: if you can run in it, you cannot land a Clipper in it.

In September 1941, a more thorough investigation of the area was conducted by PAA-Africa's Assistant Operations Manager, Karl Leuder, who confirmed that the lake was a good site for the flying boats. He also identified a nearby site for the eventual construction of a land-based landing strip for transport aircraft and this was later developed to become Benson Field. Reportedly, Karl Leuder was on Fisherman's Lake on 1 October 1941, and saw the PAA-Africa DC-3s fly over as they carried the first batch of employees from Bathurst to the main operating base in Accra.

Aerial views of Fisherman's Lake, Liberia, circa 1937. (Bridgestone/ Firestone, Inc.)

In November 1941, Pan Am's Division Engineer McVitty and Division Manager John Leslie visited the lake, and concurred that constructing a landing facility at Fisherman's Lake was feasible, and returned to the United States to plan construction.

Fisherman's Lake posed many logistical problems. It was totally isolated from the rest of Liberia. The only means of reliable surface travel between the lake and the capital city of Monrovia, 50 miles away, was by native surf boats along the Atlantic coast. A small village named Robertsport was located on the coast near the lake, but its name was deceptive. There were no port installations and all cargo had to be off-loaded from ships anchored off the coast and brought to shore by native long boats.

Much of the credit for the early success of establishing Fisherman's Lake goes to Father Harvey Simmons, O.H.C., a missionary residing in Robertsport. He obtained initial provisions of food and water for Pan Am's employees, and assisted by recruiting the local natives as laborers for the construction. According to one internal company memorandum:

> ...(Father Simmons) greatly served his country by providing housing and rendering tangible aid too extensive to be detailed here. Without him and his Mission organization, the job would have been months delayed.

Another local resident, a Dutch trader named Heugens, provided invaluable assistance to the newly-arrived Americans. He had been involved in the export of palm oil from Liberia and was soon designated as the Pan Am agent for Fisherman's Lake, responsible for ensuring that fuel and other supplies were brought by boat from Monrovia.

Two Grumman G-21A amphibians were brought to Liberia to carry passengers and cargo from Fisherman's Lake to Monrovia and Roberts Field, 40 and 80 miles, respectively.

Captain A. L. McCullough is credited with making the first B-314 Clipper landing on Fisherman's Lake in December 1941. A complete set of sea-base installations were constructed, including a dock with aircraft fueling system, two aircraft landing floats, and a patrol launch shelter. Additionally, buildings were constructed in the on-shore camp, including staff, crew and passenger quarters, dining room, maintenance shop, power house, radio transmitter building, hospital, recreation hall, and a pump house. Pan Am's Atlantic Division and PAA-Africa had a joint staff there of 17 employees. They supported the B-314 Clippers, shuttling between Brazil and Africa, and the Grumman G-21-As operating between the lake and Roberts Field.

These pictures, taken during the last two weeks of September 1942, illustrate the labor-intensive off-loading of cargo from an ocean vessel the S.S. Cathlemet. The P.S.P. sections, each weighing 80 lb., were unloaded at the Pan American floating dock in (1) local surf boats and (2) invasion barges; then (3) carried (mostly on heads), to (4) a storage point at Robertsport. The invasion barges (5) could carry 17 tons. At Benson Field (6), the P.S.P. strips were laid in echelon rows, to speed up the construction. (National Archives)

4

5

6

One of PAA-Africa's Grumman G-21As.

Benson Field

Benson Field, about two miles from the seaplane base at Fisherman's Lake, was carved out of the palm trees. U.S. Army Engineers, who arrived in Liberia in May and June of 1942, used two-man chain-saws to clear the trees and open up the landing strip. The runway consisted of a hard-packed sand surface where DC-3s could shuttle passengers and cargo from the Lake to the newly-constructed Roberts Field.

DC-3s were also used to bring cargo and passengers to the Lake to be transferred to the Boeing Clippers for the return flight to Brazil and then to the United States.

Roberts Field

Located 250 miles southeast of Freetown, Sierra Leone, Roberts Field was constructed by Pan American under the provisions of the U.S.-funded Airport Development Program (ADP). In turn, Pan American subcontracted much of the work to the Firestone Plantation Company. Construction began in 1941 and by early February 1942 Roberts Field was receiving its first large transport aircraft, even though construction was not fully completed until late in 1942.

(Top) A DC-3 prepares for departure from Benson Field. The picture is taken from the next DC-3 in line for take-off. (Bottom) Captain Donald J. Stoeger and 1st Officer Raymond Sylvester enjoying a relaxing moment at their quarters on the Firestone Plantation in Liberia in 1942. Living conditions on the plantation were more than adequate.

The landing strip was a 6,200-foot paved runway, manned by thirty PAA-Africa personnel. With the development of longer-ranged four-engined transport aircraft, it became an aviation gateway to Africa. Boeing B-314 Clipper flights decreased as the Douglas C-54s and Consolidated C-87s became available for the long-haul flights across the South Atlantic.

The PAA-Africa staff was housed in the Firestone Plantation and had access to the company's commissary and many other amenities that were not available to Pan Am staff manning other locations in Africa.

By the spring of 1942, additional Americans were arriving in Liberia, headed by a group of U.S. Army Engineers who built roads, maintained the airport at Roberts Field, cleared the site, leveled the landing strip for Benson Field, and built other wartime structures and installations in Liberia. The initial cadre of these Army engineers were black American soldiers. The Engineers established a small dock at the confluence of the Du and Farmington Rivers. They called it SNAFU dock—Situation Normal All Fouled Up—to put it politely.

SNAFU dock was the closest to Roberts Field and was therefore used to supply fuel and other bulky commodities to the airfield. Roberts Field eventually became a major air base supporting the Allies' war effort.

An aerial view of cargo off-loading at the SNAFU dock in May 1942.
Lighters carried supplies ashore from larger ships anchored off the coast.
German U-Boats operating in the area posed a significant risk to the operations.
(National Archives)

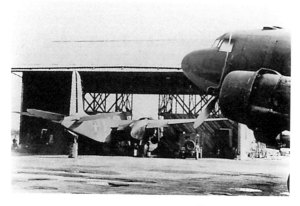

*(Top) A hangar provided some
protection from the rains in
Liberia. (National Archives)*

*(Middle) The original control
tower built at Roberts Field in
1942. (National Archives)*

*(Bottom) Barracks and
administration buildings at
Roberts Field (National
Archives)*

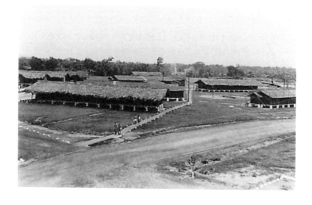

Gold Coast

In the Gold Coast, a British colony, now the independent nation of Ghana, PAA-Africa used airports at Takoradi, the main port, and Accra, the colonial capital.

Takoradi

The Gold Coast's only major seaport is located almost 600 miles east of Roberts Field, Liberia. Its airport was used by the British to trans-ship fighter aircraft from the United Kingdom to North Africa. These included Hawker Hurricanes, Supermarine Spitfires, Bristol Blenheim bombers, and Lockheed Hudsons, which arrived in crates as ship's cargo. British airmen uncrated and reassembled the aircraft and Royal Air Force (R.A.F.) pilots flew the aircraft across central Africa to Cairo.

PAA-Africa, Ltd., built three barracks and a warehouse in Takoradi, which were used in conjunction with receiving personnel and cargo through the seaport. A PAA-Africa shipping representative was assigned to handle company cargo, including frozen meats and foodstuffs. Between seven and twelve PAA-Africa employees were assigned to Takoradi, working closely with the British to assist in reassembling the British pursuit aircraft.

Accra

Accra, capital city of the Gold Coast Colony, is located just 122 miles east of Takoradi. PAA-Africa's management chose Accra to be the main operating base for the entire trans-Africa air route. As such it was developed as the largest of all the air bases along the route, with extensive support installations and amenities. By September 1942 it was home to more than 730 employees.

Pan Am's Vice President, Franklin Gledhill, first visited the airfield during his survey trip in July 1941. He considered most of the existing structures to be antiquated and requested that additional buildings be constructed. With the help of the British, PAA proceeded to build a modern airline base in Accra, including a fully operational airport and a camp for housing the PAA-Africa employees.

The PAA-Africa camp was constructed on a piece of land that overlooked the ocean, about three miles from the airfield. Living quarters were constructed and each building had about ten rooms and a bathroom. It was complete with housing, messing, maintenance, communications, operations offices, recreational, and medical facilities. The newly-arrived Americans were much impressed by the extensive use of mahogany wood in the camp.

The busy flight line at Accra. (National Archives)

Buildings, furniture, doors, and even the latrines were constructed of this wood. To the newcomers, mahogany was an exotic and expensive wood, but it was as common in West Africa as is pine or fir in America.

The history of the Accra airport began in 1920, when the British colonial government first took title to a piece of land which became the Gold Coast's first landing strip. In 1928 the landing zone was moved to a clay-based site four miles north of the town. By 1937, improvements had been made, including the construction of three runways, each 1,070 yards long and 75 yards wide. One of these had a tarred surface, the other two were gravel.

The Royal Air Force arrived in Accra in June 1941. It began immediately to construct two blocks of offices, a main store, a flight store and workshop, parachute store, oil store, roads, and a mess-hall.

By August, it was announced that Pan American Airways air crews and personnel would be arriving in Accra in large numbers. The buildings under construction for the R.A.F. were redesignated for PAA-Africa's use. The first complement of 39 personnel arrived on 1 October, to take possession on 6 October of the housing camp, with its incomplete construction projects.

During its 15-month tenure at Accra, PAA-Africa continued to improve the installations and amenities. The Americans believed that the British-built ones were inferior and had to be remodeled to meet American standards, particularly the plumbing which needed upgrading.

As the tempo of flight operations grew, additional construction projects were initiated at the airfield and at the housing camp. These included:

> *Airport Buildings:*   Extensions to existing offices, garage, and workshop, three new office buildings, including a headquarters building for the Wing and the Ferrying Command. Extensions to main store, foundation, and floors of two large steel hangars with 20,000 square yards concrete aprons; 15 prefabricated steel buildings, etc.

> *Airport Services:*   Roads, water mains, pump house sewer and septic systems, telephone and cable trenches, etc.

> *Airport Runways:*   500 ft. extension to No. 1 runway, reinforced concrete hard stand for heavy bombers, a 400-foot diameter turning semicircle at the end of runway No. 1, and paved dispersal areas for aircraft.

Camp Buildings: Pilots' mess, quarters and recreation buildings. A 50-bed hospital, eight warehouses, laundry and boiler house, three power stations, foundations, and floors for refrigerator buildings and workshops, etc.

Camp Services: One 30,000-gallon elevated water tank, sewers, and septic systems, roads, surface water drains, etc.

Ed Rose was the Airport Manager in Accra. Under his leadership, the Accra airfield functioned well as the main base for PAA-Africa. Besides acting as the terminus for a vast continental supply system, moving high-priority freight and passengers across Africa, Accra served as the headquarters for all the operating sites spread out not only over Africa, but also in the Middle East and South Asia. At one stage early in 1943, the U.S. Army had a plan to increase the size of the base at Accra to hold 32,000 U.S. military personnel, but this was never implemented.

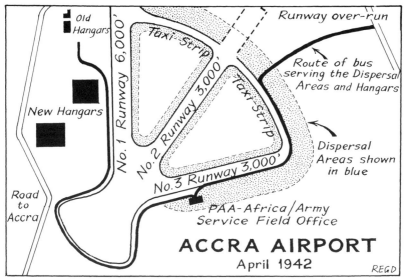

By April 1942, three runways were upgraded to a standard that would permit use by heavy bombers and transport aircraft. Heavy bombers could be parked only on the taxi strip. Other aircraft were parked mainly on both sides of No. 3 runway, and well clear of the runway intersections.

There was concern that the base might be targeted for attacks by the Germans either by air or by sea, and so slit-trenches and bomb shelters were prepared. During the initial drills of the air defense system in Accra, the men found that most of the trenches were half-filled with water and that they were already occupied by an assortment of snakes and scorpions. Thereafter, the trenches and bomb shelters were not used too often.

Nigeria

Several major airfields were operated by PAA-Africa in what is today the independent nation of Nigeria. These included sites in Lagos, Kano, and Maiduguri.

Lagos

Lagos, then capital of Nigeria, is located 251 miles east of Accra. (In recent years the capital has been relocated to the newly constructed city of Abuja.) There were two Pan Am landing areas in Lagos: a marine base and a land-plane airfield. Thus, two different organizations were operating in Lagos. The Atlantic Division, with offices in "Airways House," was handling the Boeing B-314 Clippers; while PAA-Africa, Ltd. operated the trans-Africa route and assisted with the aircraft ferry operations. With 19 station employees in Lagos, C. F. Ruegg was appointed the Senior Representative for Pan American Airways and charged with coordinating operations. Franklin Gledhill signed the appointment letter on 18 March 1942, empowering Ruegg to sign contracts and resolve all conflicts between the two organizations.

PAA-Africa's landplanes used a 2,000-foot gravel airstrip at Apappa airfield, located near the seaport of Lagos. The location of this field near the coast enabled aircraft to let down through bad weather over the water and then fly back to the shoreline, picking up visually the long breakwater which guided the pilots to the port and then to the nearby airfield. The Lagos harbor was so close to the airfield that ships docked along the pier often posed a serious obstacle to aircraft landing at Apappa.

Ferry crews returning westward through Lagos were housed in the British Army Officers' Transit Camp which was located in the Ikoyi district of town. Food at the camp was prepared under the supervision of the wife of one of the British officers. There was a swimming pool on the grounds and native drivers provided transportation for the passengers and crews to and from the airfield.

Kano

Kano, located 524 miles north of Lagos, is a northern provincial capital well known over the centuries as an important trading center. Located at the end of a Nigerian railroad running from the port at Lagos, Kano played a pivotal role in the movement of supplies and equipment required to establish PAA's infrastructure eastward across central Africa. Much of PAA-Africa's bulky cargo was shipped over the rail line as far as Kano and then either flown eastward on board PAA's transport aircraft or shipped by surface transport from Kano via road or desert track.

The airfield at Kano, which had been established by Imperial Airways late in the 1930s, was located about seven miles outside the walled city. In November 1941 Bob Nelson, the first PAA-Africa station manager at Kano, arrived and set up operations with the assistance of the R.A.F. unit already established at the field. PAA-Africa constructed four staff houses, a power plant with eight Lorimer diesels, and a 500-man Army camp. Kano was designated to be the scheduled overnight stop for westbound flight traffic between Khartoum and Accra.

News of the attack on Pearl Harbor did not reach Kano until 9 December 1941, when R.A.F. ferry pilots delivered the news as they passed through. As the traffic increased, so did the size of the PAA staff and the number of buildings constructed to support their activities. One memorable event in Kano was Opening Night for the station's new quarters and mess hall. As the electricity was turned on for the new electric ranges, it overloaded the

The flight line at Kano. (National Archives)

lines and blew the electrical power system for most of the city of Kano. Repairs were made and the power was restored, but not without some embarrassment.

Like most airfields in Africa, the runway at Kano also served the locals as a pathway to accomplish daily chores and duties. Eventually, one person was killed and several others injured during close encounters with aircraft moving on the field. The Sultan of Kano took action to solve this problem. He provided a sentinel to warn all the people of pending aircraft landings and takeoffs. Operating from a thatched hut on the field, the sentry blew a six-foot-long ceremonial horn to warn everyone that an aircraft was approaching.

Maiduguri

On 19 October 1941, PAA opened a station in Maiduguri, located approximately 308 miles east of Kano and 370 miles from the nearest rail head at Jos. All the structures at this site had to be built from scratch. Passenger and staff quarters, as well as facilities for overnight servicing of aircraft, were constructed. It was designated as the scheduled overnight stop for eastbound flight traffic between Accra and Khartoum.

The original landing strip was desert sand and poorly visible to the pilots. Many pilots inadvertently overflew the field because the runway was barely discernible from adjacent terrain. Over time, a more visible asphalt landing strip was installed.

Maiduguri was considered to be the best layover spot on the entire route. Out of this desolate terrain, PAA-Africa had developed one of the most efficiently-run stations. The food prepared by chief cook, Frank Pelican, was fit for a gourmet, and the services provided to crews and passengers alike were extraordinary. The meals were supplemented with meat and fowl hunted in the wild by the station's employees. All the aircraft maintenance work was completed outdoors at Maiduguri. The 32-member PAA staff had a pet leopard as the station's mascot.

French Equatorial Africa

Before the Second World War, and until the dissolution of its empire in Africa, the extensive French territories in the Sahara and tropical regions were designated as two main areas: French West Africa and French Equatorial Africa. PAA-Africa's staging point was in the Chad subdivision of the latter. Chad is now an independent republic.

(Top) A C-87 taxies to the parking area on the flight line at Maiduguri. (National Archives) (Middle) Roy Hackett standing on a P-40 engine during an engine change in Maiduguri. (Bottom) The leopard mascot at Maiduguri.

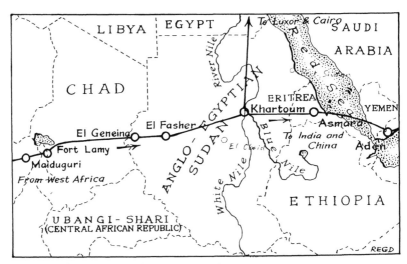

This trans-Africa route was first established by Britain's Imperial Airways in 1936, using de Havilland four-engined biplanes. The airfields were dirt strips, sometimes almost indistinguishable from the surrounding desert or savannah. PAA-Africa's main objective was to upgrade these to a standard that was compatible with wartime transports such as the C-46, C-47, or four-engined bombers.

Warehouse at Fort Lamy, where valuable cargo was stored. The word "Distillery" on the carton indicates that the Pan Am folk knew their priorities.

Fort Lamy

Fort Lamy, known today as N'Djamena, Chad, was the capital city of the Chad colony, which was then part of French Equatorial Africa. Free French Forces of General DeGaulle were in control of the city. Located 145 miles east of Maiduguri, the airfield had a brick runway with one hangar located at the end of the runway.

John Reid, Airport Manager at Fort Lamy, was one of the few PAA-Africa employees to come under direct enemy attack. In the winter of 1942, the Germans launched a single air attack on the town. Some gasoline stocks were hit, but little lasting damage was sustained.

Fort Lamy became the main source for hard liquor along the route. Some of the PAA-Africa crews discovered that the Free French officers had managed to stockpile a large quantity of Canadian Club whiskey, some 50,000 cases. This fact became known to the PAA-Africa management only after a large number of aircraft began to experience engine problems when overhead at Fort Lamy and started to make unscheduled maintenance stops at the field.

Other than the booze, Fort Lamy was one of the least attractive stops for the PAA crews. Miserable conditions resulting from a poor sanitation system and a myriad of bugs and flies encouraged air crews to keep ground time to a minimum.

Anglo-Egyptian Sudan

One of the largest, and several of the important smaller airfields on the trans-Africa air route, were in Anglo-Egyptian Sudan, now Sudan, the largest country in Africa.

El Geneina

El Geneina was one of the most isolated operating locations. Situated at the geographical center of Africa, some 497 miles east of Fort Lamy, it is located on rocky, sandy terrain at an elevation of 2,700 feet above sea level. The 12,000-foot-high Marra mountains are located about 100 miles to the southeast.

The airfield had two runways. The longest was 4,500 feet, with asphalt covering two-thirds of its surface, the shorter was 3,900 feet of gravel. A small brick run-up strip was constructed near the end of the runway to prevent the propellers from being damaged by flying gravel during engine run-up.

Ed Purcell was PAA's Station Manager at El Geneina, and in an essay he authored in 1946, he described in detail what it was like at this post.

PAA-Africa operations at El Geneina were typical of a small line station. At the outset, Geneina was regarded only as a prospective refueling and emergency stop. When the station was opened on 18 November 1941, one PAA-Africa employee, an operations representative, was assigned there. Some weeks later he was joined by a mechanic, and these two men covered the station until April, 1942. On 1 April a second ground operations man arrived, and, as the summer approached, PAA-Africa operations at Geneina grew in volume. Additional personnel were assigned, the number of aircraft handled increased, and overnights of in-transit crews and passengers became usual, instead of occasional.

Before the war, the British Imperial Airways had already built a rest house in El Geneina and this was made available to PAA crews and passengers. At one stage nine PAA employees were assigned there. The R.A.F. also had about 50 men to keep Hurricanes and Spitfires moving across Africa to the north African war zone.

In June 1942 a new PAA radio station, a beacon transmitter, and complete air-ground and point-to-point radio equipment were installed. Vehicles at the airfield included a two-ton dump truck, an emergency crash-truck, a Ford "Woodie" station wagon, and a 2,000-gallon fuel truck. All these vehi-

Conditions in El Geneina were rough. The most reliable mode of ground transport was the horse and buggy.

cles had to be driven to El Geneina and none appeared to be in prime condition when they had completed their trek across 800 miles of western Sudan's inhospitable terrain.

Joe Patrick, who found himself at El Geneina in 1942, was tasked to change an engine on an A-20 aircraft that had been grounded for a long time. Because he was working alone and had no proper hoist, he jury-rigged a wooden tripod with a block and tackle and enlisted the assistance of some of the local population to change the engine. To this day, he remembers the location as being "quite primitive in every respect."

Aviation fuel was a vital commodity at El Geneina. It had to be transported from Port Sudan, on the Red Sea, by rail through Khartoum to El Obeid, where it was placed on trucks for the 800-mile trek across desert and mountains to El Geneina. Camels had formerly been used to carry fuel in five-gallon tins, but this was discontinued because of the spillage loss rate. Purcell comments that:

> Because of fuel scarcity, and the difficulty of fuel supply, aircraft gasoline was carefully rationed; fighter convoys were refueled for flight to El Fasher only, a distance of 195 miles, and the Douglas transports received only the fuel needed for flight to Khartoum or Maiduguri. Shortage of fuel, and of accommodations, were always factors during the period of PAA-Africa operations at Geneina, but there were other shortages, besides.

Purcell also noted that stocks of water and food often ran short for those stationed in El Geneina. Vegetables and eggs were shipped in from southern Sudan, while meat and fowl were obtained by local hunting trips. Various species of antelope and gazelle, as well as guinea fowl, bustards, and other game birds, were readily available in the area; and thus hunting became a common recreation.

El Geneina was well know for its pet giraffe. Partially domesticated, it was given the run of the airfield and would venture out to the aircraft to greet the pilots. Many an airman, new to the station, and opening his cockpit window as the ground crew put in the chocks, was astonished to come face to face with a friendly giraffe.

Riding, or attempting to ride, the giraffe was great sport, although more that one prospective "giraffe jockey" was injured during attempts to mount the animal. Ed Purcell, who suffered the consequences of an attempted ride, spent four days recovering in the PAA-Africa hospital in Khartoum. At least one PAA pilot suffered a broken arm as he attempted to ride the "pet." The giraffe also created a great nuisance of itself when one day it walked through

The giraffe mascot at El Geneina. Riding was great sport—but the most exciting part was getting on board. It was a multi-step process. More than one potential "giraffe jockey" found his way to the hospital before ever finding his way to the giraffe's back.

An aerial view of El Fasher airfield. The installations were sparse and the landing strips were barely distinguishable from the surrounding desert.

the newly constructed radio beacon antenna wires, tearing them down and then running off into the desert with the wire dangling around its neck. Several men chased the animal for miles to retrieve the valuable copper wire and put the radio station back on the air.

El Fasher

El Fasher was another isolated station on the route. Located just 195 miles east of El Geneina, temperatures were often recorded at well over 120°F.

Local Sudanese helpers in front of airport operations facility at El Fasher.

Leo the Lion hamming it up with the staff at El Fasher.

Company records indicate that temperatures of 155° were not unknown. The airfield was not paved and the surface was simply a smoothed-out portion of the desert terrain. It served as an emergency landing field as well as a refueling stop for the smaller pursuit aircraft ferried across Africa. Up to eleven PAA-Africa employees were assigned to this station.

El Fasher was most famous for its mascot, "Leo the Lion," who was reportedly given, as a cub, to the R.A.F. station at El Fasher by the Governor of French Equatorial Africa. As he grew in size, Leo did a magnificent job of scaring most of the "first-timer" air crew members that came through El Fasher. He loved to walk around the flight line, grabbing onto legs and arms, trying to get the staff and air crews to play with him.

British Governor Engleson in Darfur Province, participating in a game of tennis at El Fasher on Christmas Day 1941.

Welcome to El Fasher

Leo had a way of introducing El Fasher to unsuspecting new aviators. The routine was to find some pretense to have the "new guy" on the crew leave the aircraft alone and walk to the operations building. Leo would stalk the man and pounce on him. As man and lion fell to the ground, Leo would then lick the man's face. These encounters with Leo usually resulted in a good laugh, and on many occasions soiled shorts.

Leo eventually outgrew his playful role and was taken to Khartoum and placed in the zoo. Some of the PAA employees still tell the story of how they went to visit him in Khartoum, and to the astonishment of onlookers, jumped the fence of the lion pen to pet old Leo.

There was a rather large British community at El Fasher, where both the R.A.F. and B.O.A.C. (which had succeeded Imperial Airways in 1940 as Britain's state airline) maintained men and equipment at the airfield. Also, the town served as the home of the British Governor of Darfur Province. The British and the Americans cooperated and provided mutual assistance. As seen in the photographs opposite, they worked and played together.

Khartoum

PAA-Africa officially opened its operations in Khartoum on 20 October 1941. Located some 503 miles east of El Fasher, and already a key staging point on the British route to South Africa, this became a major airport along the trans-Africa air route. Staffed with up to 86 PAA employees, it provided secondary maintenance and operational support and served as an important overnight stop for PAA crews and passengers. The airfield was located on the west bank of the Nile river in an area called Wadi Seidna, some 20 miles north of the city of Khartoum.

Living quarters were procured at the unoccupied new buildings of the Gordon Agricultural College, located near the airfield.

The airport was built by PAA-Africa and communication and maintenance services were installed. The runway proved too short for the larger B-17s and B-24s and so the whitewashed runway end-markers were repositioned further out into the desert, thus increasing the runway length and keeping the bomber pilots happy.

PAA constructed a main hangar, administration building, warehouse, large nose hangar, wells, and supplemental buildings. Living conditions were considered to be quite good. The amenities included grass tennis courts and a swimming pool, while in the city were motion picture theaters, a zoo, and two night clubs. Initially, Khartoum had been considered for possible selection to

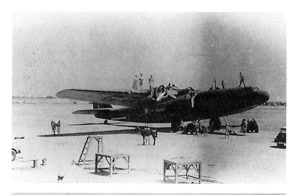

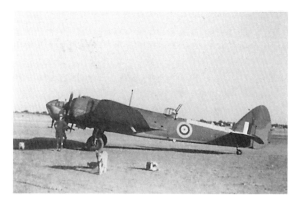

(Top) A B.O.A.C. Armstrong-Whitworth Ensign being serviced in El Fasher. These four-engined aircraft had entered service just before the beginning of the war. (Middle) A Douglas DB-7 Boston, a versatile utility aircraft used extensively at the outset of the war. (Bottom) A British Blenheim bomber and friend Leo the Lion on the flight line.

(Top) A British VickersWellesley bomber (at this time, the Wellesley held the world's long-distance air record, having flown non-stop from the Suez Canal Zone to Australia). (Middle) The Free French Air Force also visited El Fasher. Seen here is a French Farman aircraft refueling. (Bottom) A British Hawker Hurricane, one of the most famous fighter aircraft of the Second World War.

*Pete Rhodes performs a hot-air (about 120°F) inspection at Khartoum in 1941.
As soon as a hangar was constructed, all maintenance was done at night. This
aircraft had not yet received its coating of U.S. Army olive-drab paint.*

*A Pan Am C-53 crashed during take-off from Khartoum.
Everyone walked away from this one.*

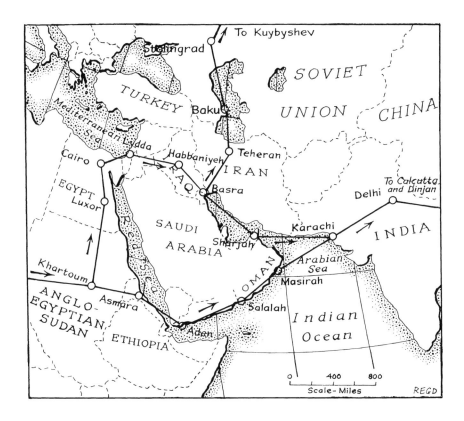

The trans-Africa route split at Khartoum. The direct route to India crossed the Red Sea to Aden and then followed the south coast of the Arabian peninsula and the Arabian Sea to Karachi. The other route followed the River Nile to join the well-established British route from the Mediterranean Sea to the Persian Gulf. At Basra, a route branched off through Persia (Iran) to take supplies and aircraft to the Soviet Union.

serve as the main operating base for PAA-Africa, but it was passed over because of the excessive daytime temperatures.

One of the unusual aspects of the Khartoum operation was that the River Nile was also used by Pan American Boeing B-314 Clippers as they passed through the area on various wartime special missions. Although these

View of a wing top of a Boeing-314 Clipper in 1941 on the River Nile. Many of Pan American's wartime "Special Missions," using the long range Clippers, made servicing stops on the river at Khartoum. Two British flying boats can be seen in the background.

were not directly affiliated with PAA-Africa, the latter was able to provide ground support. Other flying boats belonging to B.O.A.C. also routinely used the long established seaplane base.

As the pace of flight activity quickened, several accidents were recorded at Khartoum. Extreme heat and dust storms (or "haboobs") were serious impediments to operations. The heat was so severe that most of the outdoor maintenance had to be accomplished at night. Most of the aircraft departures were scheduled for first light to avoid the heat. R.A.F. reports stated that small supplies of ammunition had exploded spontaneously because of the heat.

One memorable event on the Nile occurred on 31 December 1941. Captain Eugene Fricks and his crew were crossing central Africa in a Consolidated PBY amphibian that they were delivering to the Dutch in the East Indies. An internal Pan American memorandum describes what happened:

Sliding Down the Nile
As the trip progressed, the crew became more confident and familiar with the equipment and thus were willing to make a night takeoff at

Khartoum even though the flying boat was heavily loaded with much needed ammunition for the American Volunteer Group, because by so doing considerable time could be saved.

Six flare lights were placed along the river. The crew was informed that after the last light the river's channel turned slightly to the left. Accordingly, all preparations being concluded, the engines were started and the ship began to move up the river. As the last flare was passed, a slight turn to the left was made. Suddenly, just as the boat was about to leave the water, a terrific clamor was heard and an abrupt jolt was felt. The ship stopped. Turning to McKenney (the co-pilot) Captain Fricks said, "Well, I guess we might as well turn off the motors."

"What the hell, do you want to drift down the river!" his co-pilot replied.

Handing him a flashlight, Captain Fricks said, "Well, look out for yourself, we're 200 feet up on the muddy banks in the midst of someone's bean garden."

Unfortunately, the turn in the river had been a mile further up and was not just after the last light as they had understood. Resigned to their destiny, the crew decided to spend the night aboard and attempted to get some sleep.

A couple of hours later they were "rudely" awakened by a knock on the side of the ship and voices saying, "Old Chappie, are you hurt?" "No, damn it, but you don't have to scare us to death!" the crew replied.

"How's for giving us a hand and getting us out of here?" "Oh, nothing can be done for six months. Then the river will be flooded and you can float off."

Not being satisfied at the prospects of spending the next six months on the banks of the Nile, when this ship was badly needed together with its supplies in Java, Captain Fricks and the boys unloaded the ship, rounded up Harry Rammer, Pan American Airways-Africa's local representative, Bill Newport, Chief Mechanic, and apprentice mechanic Bennen, and set to work some more American ingenuity.

Sixty natives were collected, a broken down old fire pump was borrowed from the native government, and a mud dike was built encircling the aircraft. Then, just four hours after the gang started their work, the boat, now floating in the little pond they built, was turned around to face the direction of the river. The flats along the river bank was muddied with

*(Top) A Free French Air Force Dewoitine 338 airliner-transport
being serviced at Khartoum.
(Middle) A Royal Air Force Douglas A-20 Boston.
(Bottom) Refuelling a Consolidated B-24 Liberator.*

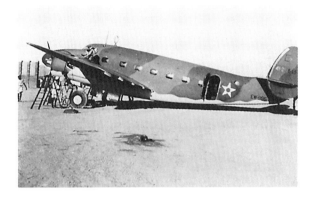

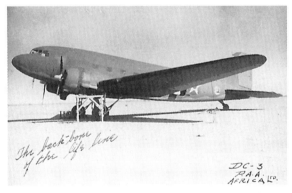

(Top) The Lockheed L-18 Lodestar was a useful twin-engined airliner used extensively in Africa during the Second World War. (Middle) Curtiss P-40 fighter aircraft en route to Burma and beyond. (Bottom) The Douglas C-47, military version of the famous DC-3, was the workhorse of the trans-Africa lifeline.

water, the engines started, given the gun and the amphibian hit the dike with such momentum that the mud was splattered in every direction. The rush of the water in the little pond carried the ship right into the river.

Upon inspection no damage had been done, no leaks could be found, so Captain Fricks called the British, requesting their cargo of incendiary ammunition be reloaded on the aircraft.

"Stop kidding us," the British replied. Well, within a few hours the ship was loaded and was again on its way to help the Dutch. An hour after their arrival at the point of destination in the Far East, this particular ship had been refueled and was off on another military mission.

PAA-Africa's personnel visited Khartoum's city center for "R&R"— relaxation and recreation. The marketplace in the adjacent city of Omdurman was famous for its "deals" in ivory, African baskets, and carvings, as well as many historical sights to see on a tour of the town.

Because of the geography of Africa and the limited range of most of the aircraft transiting the continent in 1941–1942, Khartoum saw most of the aircraft that came through the route. As illustrated on pages 70 and 71, some of the machines were somewhat unusual.

In Khartoum the route split in two different directions. One route continued north, following the Nile to Cairo, the second continued eastward to Gura, near Asmara, Eritrea, and then to India.

Another rare aircraft used on this route was the TWA Boeing-307, the Cherokee, *shown here at Khartoum on one of its regular wartime scheduled runs between Monrovia and Cairo or Aden.*

Egypt

In 1941 Egypt was an independent kingdom with British protective rights. Cairo became the major resupply point for the British forces fighting the Axis armies invading from the Italian colony, Libya, to the west. PAA-Africa used airports in two Egyptian cities.

Luxor

Luxor was a small site located 718 miles north of Khartoum on the east bank of the Nile River. It proved to be an interesting layover spot for the crews as it is the site of the famous Ancient Egyptian ruins, including the temples of Karnak and Thebes, as well as the nearby tombs in the Valley of the Kings. Luxor airport served as an emergency airfield and only nine PAA-Africa people were assigned there, residing in the Luxor Hotel. It was the initial destination for Americans who were evacuated from Cairo in July 1942.

Cairo

Cairo, 315 miles north of Luxor, was a major hub of the trans-Africa route. PAA-Africa opened shop on 29 December 1941. Most of the aircraft being ferried to the British forces in north Africa in 1941–1942 were delivered to

A full ramp at the Heliopolis Airport in Cairo. (National Archives)

During the war, the Egyptian airline, Misrair, was operating local services with de Havilland D.H. 86 four-engined biplane airliners.

the British in Cairo. PAA's transport aircraft were sent there to pick up the British and American ferry pilots and return them to Accra or Takoradi, whence the British would fly new aircraft back to Cairo, while the Americans would continue back to the United States on the Pan Am Clippers, and fly new aircraft back to Africa.

There were two main airports in Cairo: Almaza, the civilian airfield, and Heliopolis, the R.A.F. airfield. PAA-Africa operated from Almaza until late in June 1942 and then moved to the more secure R.A.F. base at Heliopolis, because of security concerns at the civilian airfield. Some Egyptians were unsympathetic to the British war effort, partly because of the basing of troops. Heliopolis airfield was just a smooth area in the desert on the northeast outskirts of the city. There were no runways, only a white painted circle in the middle of the field. The pilots would line up with the wind and land as close to the circle as they could.

The Pan American crew quarters in Heliopolis, a suburb of Cairo.

*The famous
Shepheard's Hotel in
downtown Cairo.*

The PAA crews were initially housed in the Heliopolis Hotel. Eventually, PAA-Africa obtained a nearby private villa that was used by the crews and which served as a well-equipped Staff House. Passengers were housed in hotels in downtown Cairo. These included the famous Shepheard's Hotel, as well as the Mena House, located near the Pyramids and the Giza Plateau.

Cairo was a very busy station for PAA-Africa. The seaport at Suez City, at the southern end of the Suez Canal, 40 miles to the east, was used to transfer cargo from ocean-going ships. VIP flights and other special missions routinely operated through Cairo and a Special PAA Representative was assigned to handle all non-routine operations such as liaison with the British military commanders and other Allied military personnel.

Cairo offered all the amenities the 28-member staff needed. Shopping at the Khan El Khalili suq (bazaar) was always an adventure. And for any of the staff interested in ancient Egyptian history, Cairo was almost like heaven.

Cairo was also the site of the second evacuation operation undertaken by PAA-Africa. In early July 1942, a State of Emergency was declared in Cairo as General Rommel's forces pushed the British eastward from Mersa Matruh, until held up at El Alamein.

Palestine

Before the Second World War, Palestine was a relatively peaceful part of the Middle East. Once in the Turkish Ottoman Empire, Great Britain administered it under a League of Nations mandate after the First World War. Together with Iraq (see below) the British controlled the vital area between the eastern Mediterranean and the Persian Gulf, essential for the Imperial Airways route to India.

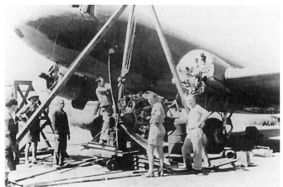

*(Top) Picture of crew changing an engine at Lydda, Palestine.
The original terminal building and control tower, shown here, was at that
time an impressive structure built for the B.O.A.C. route to the Orient. Lydda
was renamed Lod, and is known today as Ben Gurion International Airport.
(Bottom) Enlisted men from the R.A.F. pitch in to help a PAA crew to change
a C-47 engine at Lydda airport in 1942.*

Lydda,

Lydda, located about 248 miles northeast of Cairo, was the name of the British airfield located east of Tel Aviv. PAA aircraft used the field for refueling and unscheduled maintenance. Six PAA staff were assigned there. Lydda became a real crossroads of the Middle East. Many different types of aircraft from different nations could be observed on the ramp at Lydda.

Iraq

Also part of the Ottoman Empire until 1917, Iraq was at first a British-administered League of Nations mandated territory. It became independent in 1932, but Britain still retained the important R.A.F. bases at Habbaniyeh and Basra.

Habbaniyeh

This was an R.A.F. base located 514 miles east of Lydda and 40 miles west of Baghdad on the shores of Lake Habbaniyeh, in present-day Iraq. This base was unusual because the entire administrative and maintenance area was enclosed with a very high fence. Aircraft had to taxi inside the fenced area to park. A large gate was used to close off the taxi-way. Only the runway was outside the gated area. Visiting PAA crews found that the British were very uncomfortable with their Iraqi hosts. PAA had only one representative assigned there from 9 June 1942 to 14 August 1942. Aircraft usually stopped only for refueling.

Basra

By late December 1941, the PAA Representative in Cairo, James H. Smith, Jr., received the news that the extension of the PAA route to Basra was approved. Captain Kraigher flew the first survey flight early in January 1942. Initially, PAA-Africa had an agreement with the U.S. War Department to fly three trips a week between Cairo and Basra.

The airfield at Basra was located close to the Tigris River, 313 miles east of Habbaniyeh. The severe heat caused problems for arriving and departing aircraft. Temperature readings of 124°F were common. The heat and the resulting thermals caused havoc with aircraft attempting to land over the water on to the airfield. Many pilots had to go around because they arrived too fast and floated over the runway—the aircraft just did not want to land.

*The published flight schedule
from Egypt to Iraq and Iran.*

PAA-Africa, Ltd. set up a
40-man, prefabricated air-condi-
tioned housing unit that they had
purchased from the Standard Oil
Company. Eight employees were
assigned to Basra, including Frank
Pelican, the chef from Maiduguri,
who was transferred. After
Frank's arrival the quality of the
food prepared in the mess
improved markedly. He was a
welcome sight for the PAA pilots
from Accra, as they passed
through the region.

PAN AMERICAN AIRWAYS-AFRICA, LTD.

EGYPT -- IRAQ -- IRAN

Supplementary Schedule   Effective Friday, June 5, 1942

GMT Fri.	Miles	Douglas DC-3 Equipment		GMT Sun.
4:00	0	Lv. Cairo, Egypt	Ar.	10:45
8:40	765	Ar. Habbaniyeh, Iraq	Lv.	6:05
9:10		Lv. Habbaniyeh, Iraq	Ar.	5:35
9:40	835	Ar. Baghdad, Iraq	Lv.	5:05
10:00		Lv. Baghdad, Iraq	Ar.	4:45
11:45	1111	Ar. Basra, Iraq	Lv.	3:00
Sat.				Sat.
3:00		Lv. Basra, Iraq	Ar.	9:00
5:30	1523	Ar. Tehran, Iran	Lv.	6:30

NOTE: All hours indicated above are GMT. All schedules and routes
shown above are subject to change without notice.

For use of Pan American Airways personnel only - not for publication.

dr.

PAA hired Mosh Saleh, a local citizen, as an interpreter and jack-of-all-
trades. He became a legend as he assisted PAA-Africa personnel in everything
from buying Persian carpets to lending them money.

Iran

In pre-war days, Iran was called Persia, a monarchy ruled by the Shah, and
until the 1920s, a poor country, noted for its carpets. The discovery of rich oil
deposits changed its economy, and with growing economic strength, it exerted
sovereignty over its own territory and the Persian Gulf with some severity.
The British Imperial
Airways was not
permitted to operate its
route to India through
Persia. But the onset of
the Second World War
changed everything.

*A camel-powered cart,
seen in Karachi in 1942.*

Teheran

In May 1942, the U.S. Department of State and the Soviet Government nego-
tiated a once-a-week flight between Cairo and Kuybyshev or Moscow in the
Soviet Union. The diplomats agreed that PAA-Africa would fly cargo on the
Cairo to Teheran leg and the Russians would fly the leg from Teheran to
Kuybyshev or Moscow. These missions went to Teheran to pick up the U.S.
Army ferry pilots and return them to West Africa for the first leg of their trip
back to the United States. Additionally, diplomats, diplomatic mail, and cargo
were transported to Russia on these missions.

Between 1 June 1942 and 19 October 1942 PAA-Africa ran the operation into the Ghale Morghi airport located some 410 miles north of Basra, and
40 miles outside the city of Teheran. The field was shaped like a wagon wheel
with crisscrossed runways, and a taxiway circled the entire field. Flying into
Ghale Morghi was very difficult because of the high mountains located in the
immediate vicinity. The Pan Am aircraft did not have oxygen and the pilots
had to fly through the mountain passes at about 12,000 feet. Just north and
east of the field the mountains rose to more than 18,000 feet. PAA pilots were
surprised to find so many Russians at this Iranian airfield, and Russian guards
were usually put in place to watch the aircraft while they were on the ground.

India

For two centuries, India had been Great Britain's "Jewel in the Crown," a
large sub-continent of great natural wealth, and from which the colonial
power learned to drink tea, to import cotton, and to use cheap labor.
Comprising dozens of different ethnic groups and scores of languages and
religions, India finally gained its independence in 1950. Until then, the original Indian Empire under the British extended across much of southern Asia,
but it was dismembered. Burma seceded from the British Commonwealth in
1948, and Pakistan (including East Pakistan, later Bangladesh), Ceylon, and
the Maldive Islands: all broke away from India.

Karachi

On 12 April 1942, Karachi became the official end of the line of the PAA-
Africa air route. But in fact, Karachi was not always the end of the line. As
the Japanese continued to advance through Burma and China, missions flew
eastward well beyond Karachi. PAA-Africa aircraft and crews passed through
Karachi as they supported emergency resupply missions into China in April

1942, evacuated Burma in May 1942, and supplied airlift support across the "Hump" through 1944.

The airfield was located 19 miles outside of the city. The airport infrastructure was very good. Major repairs were completed in the hangars at the airfield. PAA manned this site with nine employees. In July 1942 the PAA staff included Airport Manager Phil Brown, Operations Representative Jay Lodwick, and Maintenance Repairmen Bill Newport and J. J. Patrick.

Karachi was also a layover site where the air crews could do some sightseeing and shopping. Crews were normally housed at either the Carleton or the Killarney Hotels in downtown Karachi.

New Delhi, Calcutta, and Dinjan

On 24 February 1942, Pan American Airways' office in New York published a special press release as Captain Goyette landed his DC-3 in Calcutta. For Pan American, this was the first time its air routes completely encircled the globe (even though the Pacific segments were suspended, and it still could not cross the United States). From Calcutta, PAA could connect with China, using its subsidiary China National Airline Corporation (C.N.A.C.), for connections (at least on the map) through the Pacific region all the way back to the continental United States.

The airfields at New Delhi, Calcutta, and Dinjan were used extensively during the April–May 1942 emergency airlift missions into China and Burma. Most of the wartime supplies sent to China in support of the American Volunteer Group (A.V.G.) and C.N.A.C. passed through these Indian airfields.

Oman

As an independent sultanate, Oman, located on the eastern extremity of the Arabian peninsula, had signed a series of friendship treaties with the British, with whom they had maintained close ties from the early 1800s.

Salalah

Salalah airfield, an isolated outpost located in the south of Oman, was maintained by the R.A.F. to support the operation of several Hurricane fighter aircraft based there.

On 6 June 1942, a six-man American staff arrived to establish the PAA-Africa station at Salalah. The staff included Billy McDeavett, Station Manager; Tex Middleton, Radio Engineer; Gus Bergstrom, Radio Operator;

Living conditions were quite spartan for the PAA-Africa personnel assigned to Salalah. "Cookie" is seen here, checking over his menu for the day.

Tommy O'Keefe, Chief Mechanic; Joe Hughes, Mechanic; and "Cookie" Lidz, chief cook. These men were simply dropped off on the sands from a DC-3, along with a jeep, a couple of tents, a generator, a refrigerator, and some supplies. The DC-3 then left for the return trip to Accra. They were told to establish the station from scratch, and received some assistance from the 35-man R.A.F. unit stationed at the airfield.

The runway at Salalah was nothing but a designated area on the sandy terrain. The sand runway was marked with whitewashed stone markers—two at each end of the runway. PAA-Africa pilot Dwight Shrum tells the story about one occasion when he had difficulty locating the runway at Salalah. After making a couple of low passes, Shrum thought he spotted the runway. There appeared to be a large number of people on the field, but they gradually moved aside and created just enough room to land the aircraft. Shrum's landing was uneventful. But, during the landing rollout he noticed another pile of white stones. He then realized that he had just rolled onto the real runway—only after completing the landing. There was no visual difference between the runway and the adjacent desert sands. Later, the runway sand at Salalah was mixed with camel dung to harden and stabilize the landing surface. This had the added benefit of making the runway a little more visible. During periods of bad weather, the PAA ground crews fired rocket flares from a beach area located more than a mile from the runway. The flares directed the pilots to a turn point aligned with the airfield. On one such occasion, PAA's Joe Hughes tried to launch one of the rocket flares, but it was a dud. A second rocket was prepared and launched, but by this time, the aircraft was right overhead the launch site.

When PAA Captain Johnny Warren finally landed the aircraft, the first thing he wanted to do was scalp the fellow who had almost shot down his aircraft. The delayed rocket reportedly passed between the right engine and the fuselage of his DC-3. After a quick explanation, all was forgiven.

There was no seaport at Salalah. Aviation fuel was delivered from ships that were anchored off the coast. Fifty-five-gallon barrels were rolled off the ships into the sea and local swimmers would swim the barrels onto the shore.

The station often ran low on drinking water. More than one PAA-Africa air crew shared on-board water supplies with the men in Salalah.

On 1 August 1942, the militarization of the air route had begun and the PAA representatives were replaced by U.S. Army personnel.

Promotions at Salalah

Harry Jenkins tells a story about Salalah; after militarization seven U.S. Army servicemen were still manning this station. One day General Hap Arnold, Chief of the Army Air Corps, made an unscheduled stop there in his B-17. After spending some time on the ground for refueling and seeing firsthand the austere conditions under which these men had to operate, he directed that they all be promoted one rank. 1st Lt. Bill Pike and his six enlisted men soon received their promotions.

Aden

The British crown colony of Aden, modern-day Yemen, located on the tip of the Arabian peninsula, at the southern end of the Red Sea, was an important refueling stop for British ships. As a British Protectorate, it was situated at a very strategic site.

A welcoming committee greets a Pan American C-47 in Ethiopia. Three armed troops were there to ensure correct protocol.

By early 1942, two PAA personnel were assigned to this station, Station Manager Turner Austin and Acting Chief of Maintenance Joe Hughes (the same fellow with the flares in Salalah). Additionally two U.S. Army Air Corps Officers were assigned to Aden. They all resided with British R.A.F. Officers in the British living quarters, where living conditions were quite pleasant. Each man had a private room with shower and washroom. House boys took care of their needs, including meals served in the large officers' mess. When transiting Aden, the PAA air crews would join their colleagues at the Officers' Club. The only thing to complain about in Aden was the quality of the food. The camel steaks were always tough.

PAA-Africa ran a schedule of one or two daily flights, passing both east and west through Aden. With this frequency, some of the PAA men found that they could make a day trip to Gura. This was significant as the Douglas Company base there boasted the only soda fountain along the trans-Africa route. Real ice cream sodas and candy bars were readily available and well worth the six-hour round trip flight.

Eritrea

Established as an Italian colony during the "scramble for Africa," Eritrea was one of the first Axis casualties of the Second World War. It became part of Ethiopia after hostilities ended, but became an independent republic in 1993.

Two airports in Eritrea were used by Americans during the Second World War. PAA-Africa established a small operation at Asmara, the capital. The Asmara airfield was situated in the Choke Mountains at an elevation of 7,500 feet above sea level and was the site of a small PAA-Africa station.

The Douglas Aircraft Company constructed a huge aircraft repair facility and airport, at Gura, southwest of Asmara, and just 5,000 feet above sea level. PAA crews ferried many war-weary B-24s and P-40s from north Africa to Gura for repairs and scheduled depot maintenance. PAA-Africa had eight employees there living in relative luxury, as the depot had a canteen which sold many American-style products, including fresh milk and ice cream.

Flight Operations

As a pilot you must always consider flying in the desert
to be exactly like flying over the ocean.
                              —Egyptian Air Force General (circa 1979)

Who better to operate aircraft over the ocean-like desert of Africa than the company that pioneered flight operations over the Pacific Ocean in the late 1930s? The desert was just one of the many challenges facing the men of PAA-Africa as they began to fulfil the terms of their contractual agreements. Jungles, swamps, disease, heat, severe storms, and mountains rounded out a list of environmental challenges faced, on an almost daily basis, by the men of PAA-Africa.

The Fleet

The Douglas DC-3

Under the terms of the contract, PAA-Africa Ltd. was to receive 20 multi-engined cargo aircraft to initiate the air route in Africa. This fleet consisted mostly of Douglas twin-engined DC-3 transports. From an initial allotment of six, the fleet grew to a total of seventy-nine aircraft that were used during PAA-Africa's operational lifetime. The aircraft were provided by the U.S. Government, which obtained them through impressment action, taking possession from the domestic fleets of U.S. airline companies, or right off the assembly line as production rates increased in late 1941 and early 1942. The U.S. airlines that lost aircraft included Eastern, TWA, Northwest, United, American, Pennsylvania Central, City Service Company, Canadian Colonial, and even Pan American itself. All were obliged to transfer aircraft to the Federal Government, which in turn assigned them to PAA-Africa to support the high-priority mission in Africa.

The Douglas aircraft came in various configurations. A few civilian models were DSTs (Douglas Sleeper Transports) with sleeper accommodation and small upper fuselage windows. Most were DC-3s, DC-3Bs, and two C-68s (the only two made by Douglas). The military versions of this same model were referred to as C-53s, C-53Bs, and C-47s. Most of the military aircraft were C-47s, which had the larger two-panel cargo door opening on the port side of the aft fuselage and reinforced cabin flooring to support the tying down of heavier cargo. They started to come off the assembly line in November 1941. The first aircraft to arrive in Africa were unpainted and are seen in photographs with polished aluminum exteriors. After the United States entered the war, they were painted in the U.S. Army's olive drab paint scheme, with military markings.

The standard passenger version of the DC-3 was authorized to operate in the United States at a maximum gross weight of 26,000 lb. Because of the high priority of wartime cargo, PAA authorized its crews to fly the aircraft at 31,000 lb. gross weight while operating in Africa. This was a calculated trade-off; at this weight the aircraft could not maintain level flight on one engine.

Not all the aircraft systems needed to be maintained in Africa. The rubber de-icing boots fitted to the leading edges of the wings deteriorated rapidly in the African heat and were removed. Likewise, the alcohol reservoirs for the window and propeller de-icing systems were also inoperative. These items were not critical for flights across Africa, but they were needed—and sorely missed—by the air crews flying over the Himalayan mountains of northern India in April–May 1942. Autopilots were another aircraft system that were mostly inoperative on the PAA DC-3 fleet. That was until PAA pilot Harry Jenkins made a stop in Eritrea and inadvertently found that the Douglas Aircraft representatives, based at the newly-constructed repair depot in Gura, had a large stock of new DC-3/C-47 auto-pilots. Jenkins mentioned this to his boss, PAA's Chief Pilot, Captain Kristofferson, and over the next several months most of the Accra aircraft made landings at Gura and obtained new auto-pilots. To have an operating auto-pilot was a real treat for the PAA- Africa pilots.

The Grumman G-21A Goose

PAA-Africa's fleet also included two Grumman G-21A Goose twin-engined amphibian aircraft. They were obtained from two wealthy Americans, Boris Sergievske and James Donahue, in 1937 and 1941 respectively. One of the Grummans arrived in Africa early in December 1941 as deck cargo on the *S.S. Santa Paula*. The aircraft was put ashore in Freetown, Sierra Leone, where it was reassembled by PAA-Africa's staff and flown to Fisherman's Lake in Liberia.

The Grummans were used almost exclusively in Liberia to transport passengers and cargo between the marine base at Fisherman's Lake and the landplane base at Roberts Field, located about 80 miles to the southeast. They were the only means of transporting passengers and cargo between the two sites. On at least one occasion one of them went to Sudan to assist in a search-and-rescue mission.

This Grumman G-21 Goose was sent to El Fasher to assist in the search for the lost flight of P-40s.

The Grumman G-21As worked well for the limited amount of passenger and cargo traffic at the start of the operation. But, as the flow of traffic dramatically increased in 1942, it became more difficult for them to keep up. They were used extensively until Benson Field, the new landplane field, was constructed adjacent to Fisherman's Lake. PAA's DC-3s and C-47s were then able to take over the job of hauling passengers and cargo between Fisherman's Lake and Roberts Field.

The Grummans were flexible in their amphibious role. As well as operating the Fisherman's Lake–Roberts Field "shuttle," they were used to ferry personnel to the lagoon outside the capital city Monrovia. They were sometimes used to support the travel requirements of Liberian government officials.

The Lockheed Hudson

The Operations Department's Flight Summary Report for the month of April 1942 also lists seven Lockheed aircraft, believed to be Hudsons, in PAA-Africa's fleet, which were used to support both scheduled and non-scheduled

One of the PAA Grummans on the lagoon in Monrovia, in 1942.

chartered missions. One was used as a "mother ship" in the ferry operations of P-40s across Africa.

During 1941–1942 aircraft were constantly shuffling into and out of PAA-Africa's fleet. The U.S. Army Air Corps kept moving aircraft from the factories in the United States to different units in the field, including those of the Royal Air Force and the U.S. Army's Air Transport Command. When PAA's contract finally expired in December 1942, all the aircraft assigned to PAA-Africa were transferred either to the R.A.F. in Cairo, Karachi, or Freetown; to the U.S. Army's Air Transport Command in Accra or Karachi; to the China National Aviation Corporation (C.N.A.C.); or to the U.S. Army Depot in Gura, Eritrea. [See Appendix B for a complete fleet list.]

Flight Activities

As mentioned earlier, Accra was selected to be the main operating base in Africa for PAA. All flight activities were initiated at Accra. The administrative headquarters was located there as well as the main crew base, and most of the major maintenance was performed on the aircraft in Accra.

In October 1941 Operations Manager George Kraigher conducted a route survey across Africa using two DC-2s and one DC-3. The three aircraft left Accra on 9 October and upon arrival in Khartoum, the two DC-2s were delivered to the British R.A.F. and the lone DC-3 continued on to Cairo. The R.A.F. used the two DC-2s to resupply the British outpost on Malta. The PAA DC-3 returned to PAA-Africa's main operating base in Accra to begin routine flights. On 23 October, C.E. Shoemaker, Jr., Traffic Manager for PAA-Africa, reported back to headquarters in New York that he had, "... visited every proposed city on the route except Freetown and Monrovia, the airports there being not yet completed." He indicated his concern over the need to develop a system of priorities for passengers and cargo with the various government agencies, both American and British. He praised the British for providing "... every assistance...," as he traveled along the route.

"First Flight" became a rather commonplace term during the early days of operations in Africa. The first scheduled flight began on 22 October 1941. Senior Check Pilot Captain Frank Glen and his co-pilot, Grover Furr, left Accra on the first scheduled round-trip mission to Khartoum. By December 1941, PAA-Africa, Ltd. had received approval from the U.S. Army to extend the route to Basra. George Kraigher made the first flight to Basra.

The principal categories of flight activity fell into one of the following: Scheduled, Non-scheduled, Extra Schedule, Charter, Survey, Training, Test, and Emergency.

Scheduled Transport Operations

The principal mission assigned to PAA-Africa was to establish air transport operations across Africa. The contract stated that PAA-Africa would carry:

> (a) Such personnel, facilities, tools, materials and supplies (in addition to personnel, equipment, materials and supplies required for the Trans African Route) as may be required for the processing, repair, servicing and operation of aircraft and other defense articles being furnished by the Government (U.S.) to the British Government pursuant to the aforesaid Act; and (b) Other passengers and cargo to the extent that the remaining carrying capacity of the aircraft being operated by it shall permit after giving priority to the carriage of the personnel and cargo referred to in clause (a) of this paragraph (3).

Once a qualified Pan Am transport pilot arrived in Accra he could expect to receive a local checkout by one of the senior PAA-Africa pilots, such as "Brick" Maxwell or Henry Kristofferson. After completing "three bounces" (touch-and-go landings and takeoffs) in the local traffic pattern, the newly-arrived pilots would join the line and start as co-pilots on the route.

George Kraigher established a series of standard operating procedures and guidelines for the pilots. These included: always use the three-point landing method with the DC-3, all flights to be in daylight and in visual flying conditions (this was later modified), and everyone abide by a gentleman's agreement that you did not overtake a Pan Am pilot who was sitting on the ground waiting for weather to improve.

By the end of March 1942, 80 PAA-Africa pilots were on the job in Africa flying a fleet of 32 transport aircraft. PAA should have had more than 120 pilots to maintain the standard ratio of two crews per aircraft. The pilot shortage continued to be a problem for the company during its entire period of operations in Africa.

In June 1942, the Maintenance Superintendent in Accra sent a three-page memorandum to the Chief of Line Service, giving step-by-step instructions for "Line Duties and Run Up Procedures."

Aircraft Ferry Operations

Pan American Air Ferries, Inc., another subsidiary of Pan American, had the principal mission to perform ferry flights across the South Atlantic and Africa.

But PAA-Africa, Ltd. was given the task to provide a supporting role, providing pilots, crews to assemble aircraft, and ground and support services. The contract specified that PAA-Africa:

> ... shall, at all points along the route between Bathurst, Gambia and the East African Terminal Point, which are terminal or intermediate points on air transport services operated by African (PAA-Africa, Ltd.), cause Ferries (Pan American Air Ferries, Inc.) to be provided with all ground radio, meteorological, maintenance and operations services required, and to that end will make fully available to Ferries the ground facilities and organizations ... and will cause Ferries to be supplied at such points with such gasoline, oil and other supplies as Ferries may require in order to perform the ferry services contemplated by this contract.

The number of British aircraft arriving at the airfield in Takoradi began to increase dramatically. The R.A.F. began to use aircraft carriers, operating off the coast of Africa, to deliver large numbers of pursuit-type aircraft, flying them from the ships directly to Takoradi and Accra. The R.A.F.'s own ferry operations between Takoradi and Cairo began to back up and PAA-Africa was asked to provide pilots to assist in ferrying the aircraft to Egypt. Critically short of pilots, the British had no problem in enticing the civilian pilots of PAA-Africa to fly the aircraft. Most of the them were eager to get into the cockpit of those high-powered fighting machines. Ed (Ran) McKane was one of the PAA pilots asked to fly Hawker Hurricanes to Cairo. He received a 45-minute cockpit check and was cleared for flight after taxying around the airfield for a few minutes.

Brigadier General Harold L. George, of the U.S. Army's Air Force's Ferrying Command, had a motto for his units conducting aircraft ferry operations. It read: "Deliver the airplane safely—if not today, then tomorrow." General George stated that, "An airplane damaged, or 'smashed-out' contributes to the objective of our enemies just as definitely as though it were destroyed in combat." By May 1942, PAA-Africa's John Yeomans had adopted General George's motto.

As more British pilots became available, the need for PAA pilots to fly the British fighter aircraft diminished, but as they had now acquired much more flight experience in Africa than the young R.A.F. and U.S. Army pilots, the PAA pilots began flying in "mother" ships, leading the formations of fighter aircraft across Africa to Cairo. Douglas DB-7s or Bristol Blenheims

Lt. General Harold L. George
(National Archives)

served as navigational lead aircraft for the pursuit aircraft to follow on their way to Cairo.

The pursuit aircraft ferried across Africa were painted with a white rectangle on the spine of the fuselage, aft of the cockpit, to assist rescue crews in locating downed aircraft along the route. It showed up well to the crews in the search aircraft flying over the featureless desert or semi-desert terrain.

PAA-Africa pilots also led convoys of American P-40s across Africa to Cairo and other destinations in the Middle East and Asia. Using Douglas A-20s, Martin A-30s (Baltimores), Lockheed Hudsons and Venturas, and DC-3s they would lead the fighter aircraft by providing navigational and radio services. Larger numbers of American P-40s started to arrive in Accra as the U.S. Army began to use U.S. Navy aircraft carriers, operating off the coast of Africa, to deliver the aircraft. During the 25 June 1942 meeting of the Combined Chiefs of Staff in Washington, General Marshall advised his British counterparts that "Admiral King had approved the use of the *U.S.S. Ranger* to ferry more P-40s to Takoradi whence they could be flown to Cairo."

On at least two occasions American aircraft were delivered to West Africa using a U.S. Navy aircraft carrier. In May 1942, and then again in July, deliveries took place with about 70 P-40 aircraft arriving in Accra on each occasion. In May pilots from the A.V.G. in China came to Accra to receive aircraft, which they then flew back to China.

A "Pink P-40," viewed through a cabin window of a DC-3. Many P-40s and B-24s were camouflaged using Sand #49 paint, which reflected the red hues of the desert and gave the aircraft a pinkish appearance. Pilots of these aircraft were often razzed for flying pink planes.

Flight Conditions

No matter what the purpose of any particular flight (transport or ferry mission), or the type of aircraft being flown (P-40s, DC-3s, etc.), all of the PAA pilots shared the common experiences of flying in the rather harsh African environment. All flight activities in Africa were influenced by some rather distinctive factors. These included:

Reliance on "Dead Reckoning" (DR) Navigation

Pilots were forced to rely on the oldest method of aerial navigation known as "Dead Reckoning." Applying drift correction and variation to magnetic heading and determining distance from the point of departure, based on winds aloft, ground speed and time: these were the principal methods available to pilots to navigate across Africa. Visual flight navigation by map reading was difficult for several reasons. Few navigational maps were available. Some

General George Marshall at work in his office in Washington in November 1941. (National Archives)

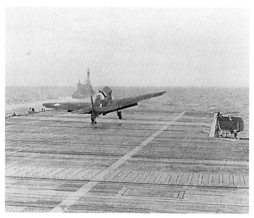

An American P-40 launches from the deck of the USS Ranger, *somewhere off the coast of West Africa on 10 May 1942. 68 P-40s arrived in Accra that day. Many of the PAA staff at Accra thought they were under enemy attack as these aircraft began arriving unannounced. A second delivery of P-40Fs, also using the* USS Ranger, *took place in July 1942. (National Archive)*

pilots used maps torn out of the pages of National Geographic magazine. Each pilot would develop his own set of visual ground reference points, which worked well only if the visibility was good enough to see them.

Late in 1941, two of PAA-Africa's pilots, Charles R. Heffner and Harry D. Jenkins, were assigned to Kano on temporary duty (TDY) for six weeks. While there, they repeatedly flew round-trip cargo missions between Kano and Khartoum. They quickly became the "resident experts" on flying over the most difficult portion of the trans-Africa route to navigate. While making the repeated flights, they noted the prevailing winds, and annotated their maps with visual checkpoints. They then shared this information with the other PAA-Africa pilots. Without radio aids for navigation, such shared observations were critical for safe flight across Africa.

Eventually, more detailed air navigational maps were obtained by the PAA pilots. Most of these were reproductions of British aeronautical charts, reproduced mainly by the U.S. Army's War College in Washington, D.C., for the U.S. Army Air Corps. The British maps, drawn to a scale of 1:2,000,000, were produced by the Geographical Section, General Staff, and published by the War Office in London. By early 1942, the Survey Directorate, H.Q. Tenth Army, began publishing maps which were then reproduced by the 1 Indian Field Survey Company. These were also used by the pilots of PAA-Africa.

Even armed with the better maps, PAA pilots were still required to use dead reckoning procedures. Ground references for visual navigation could not always be relied upon because of frequent poor visibility in the desert regions of Africa.

Jebel Bara Simbil, referred to as "Camel's dick" by the PAA pilots, was one of a few good visual check points used by the pilots to navigate along the route in western Sudan.

The Harmattan

During the months of December through March, the winds over the Sahara Desert stir up huge amounts of desert sand and dust, which then spread to the south on the prevailing winds and make life difficult for man and beast. This is especially true for pilots. The haze can be very thick and noticeable up to altitudes as high as 10,000 to 15,000 feet. The particles of sand and dust virtually destroy a pilot's "slant range" visibility. Overhead a runway at 10,000 feet, a pilot can look straight down and see the ground. But if he has to look downward at an angle, his visibility is restricted to just a couple of hundred feet, or even less. During these conditions, a pilot could receive an apparently contradictory weather report that would state, "Ceiling unlimited with visibility zero."

PAA-Africa devised its own "close-in procedures" to help pilots to counter this condition. They would use a standardized turning procedure, based on a specified heading and time, in an attempt to align the aircraft with the runway. With some luck, they would be able to see just enough of the airfield to complete a landing. If not, they would have to find somewhere else to land.

Haboobs or Sandstorms

Haboobs are localized sandstorms which can hit without warning and with winds that can reach hurricane velocity. These storms are frequently observed in Sudan. Haboobs can be seen as huge vertical walls of sand, hundreds of feet high and several miles wide, rolling through the desert in Central Africa (see photo on page 94). The duration of these storms is usually just a couple of hours. Aircraft takeoffs and landings would have to cease during these storms. One American Army Colonel, trying to explain a Haboob, told his friend that:

When one is coming up you bolt the windows, lock the door, stuff rags and papers in the crevices, crawl into bed and pull the sheets and blankets over your head. That way you get only a half inch of sand inside the sheets.

Arriving aircraft would have to hold at altitude until the storm passed or find an alternate landing place.

Both of these sand-related phenomena had other negative effects on the aircraft. Engine air filters would clog with sand particles and result in reduced engine power, rough operation, and eventually lead to engine shut-down. The airborne sand would pit the cockpit windows and make the pilots' visibility, already degraded by the refraction of the sunlight off of the sand particles, even worse. Additionally, the airborne sand particles did a nice job of sand-blasting the paint right off the aircraft.

Heat

Excessive heat in the African desert took its toll both on man and machine. Dehydration was a serious problem for the PAA maintenance workers who had to complete all their work outdoors. In the bright African sun, metal parts often became too hot to touch with a bare hand. The DC-3s had inertial starters and their switches had to be held down for 30 to 45

A wall of sand approaching the PAA camp at Khartoum.
You can run, but you cannot hide from a Haboob.

seconds during the engine start sequence. Pilots had to use handkerchiefs or other pieces of clothing to keep their fingers from burning.

Initially, all aircraft maintenance was accomplished outdoors during daylight hours at Accra, and the heat of the day exacerbated the already austere working conditions. The disease-carrying mosquitoes were so dangerous in the evenings that all night-time outdoor work was discouraged. Not until 1942 was the first of several large hangars constructed to permit work indoors and out of the sun.

Thunderstorms

West Africa is notorious for its tropical storms. While these are usually localized, they created the need for extended holding or diversions to alternate fields. Additionally, these storms made for some very bumpy rides for low flying transport and fighter aircraft. For most PAA crews, there was no way for the DC-3 to climb over the really bad weather, and at least one DC-3 did sustain serious structural damage.

Other Hazards

Friendly Fire

Friendly fire was a major concern of the PAA-Africa pilots. A "colors of the day" flare system was established to identify aircraft positively as "Friend or Foe." The air crews had to fire colored flares to identify themselves to the defenders on the ground. But the flare system was wrought with problems as crews continuously found themselves in situations where the codes they had been issued were wrong; or because of some earlier breach of security or German attack, the colors had been changed without notifying the arriving air crews. This was a critically serious concern when flying over the city of Cairo and over the Suez Canal.

American civilian air crews were particularly gun-shy about arriving in Cairo. By July 1942, the Germans were advancing and there had already been several German bombing raids made on the city. The British air-defense gun crews were edgy and likely to shoot first, and ask questions later. Therefore, for Pan Am aircraft arriving from the south, the standard procedure was to fly only ten feet above the water of the River Nile, just missing the sails of the feluccas (Nile riverboats with sails), then, upon reaching the city, turn east, pop up over one particular mosque, staying close to the rooftops of the buildings, and land at Heliopolis airfield as fast as possible before the defenders reacted.

British air defense forces also established a ten-mile-wide security corridor along the entire length of the Suez Canal. To ensure safe passage, aircraft flying in this corridor were to be at an altitude of 1,000 feet and have their landing gear down. But because the British forces continued to fire on the aircraft, even though the crews followed the correct safe passage procedures, most Pan Am pilots flew over the canal at an altitude of about ten feet, so that the anti-aircraft artillery could not be aimed and fired at them.

There was one report of a Pan American aircraft being shot down by a British Beaufighter. A DC-3 tried to leave Cairo shortly after a German air attack and the Beaufighter fired upon the American aircraft, thinking it was part of the attacking force.

Fort Lamy, Chad, was another station where incidents of "friendly fire" occurred. After a German bombing attack early in 1942, several PAA-Africa aircraft were fired upon—luckily without effect. Pilots reported that the air-defense guns continued to be aimed directly at them even while they rolled out after landing.

Hostile Enemy Fire

Both Fort Lamy and Cairo were bombed by German aircraft during PAA-Africa's tenure in the region. During one of the night-time Heinkel 111 and Junkers 88 bombing raids on Heliopolis airfield, PAA pilots Milo Bacon and Dwight Shrum watched from the roof of the PAA Staff House, which was

A co-pilot's view of the Suez Canal in 1942. PAA pilots worried about Safe Passage Procedures when flying over the Canal Zone.

located about half a mile from the airport. Next day they found four holes in their airplane, which had to be repaired before their next flight.

Several PAA crews reported that shore batteries of anti-aircraft guns fired on their aircraft as they passed off the coast of the Vichy French-held territory in West and Central Africa.

DC-3s Fighting Back

Although the cargo aircraft flown by PAA-Africa were unarmed, a couple of incidents almost turned the tables on the enemy. Dave Farabough, returning to Accra from Bathurst, was flying low over the water off the coast of Vichy territory to avoid pro-German anti-aircraft guns. Without warning he flew directly over a gathering of several German submarines, apparently tied together on the surface, holding what appeared to be some type of conference. Both sides were caught by surprise. The Germans sprang to action as they prepared to dive, thinking that bombs would be dropped at any moment. The American air crew was sure that they would be subjected to lethal gun fire. But not a shot was fired.

Off the coast of Dahomey (now Benin) an allied merchant vessel was coming under surface gun attack by a German U-Boat. A DC-3 passed the scene and returned to make several simulated strafing runs on the German boat. The U-Boat crew submerged to evade the aerial attack and the merchant vessel sped away safely. Initial reports of this action indicated that this may have been a PAA-Africa crew that made the passes over the U-Boat.

Rescue Missions

The rescue of downed air crews and their aircraft was an almost constant endeavor for the men of PAA-Africa. By late 1941, single-engined fighters were dropping out of the African skies at an alarming rate. Most of the pilots of the ill-fated flights were lost over featureless terrain and ran out of fuel. The standard procedure was to make a forced landing, as to locate flat terrain with a hard packed surface was not too difficult. With gear up, engines off, and little fuel remaining, most pilots were able to walk away from their aircraft after a successful forced landing, and were often assisted by friendly Africans. But in a couple of incidents, in East Africa and on the Arabian peninsula, downed pilots were mistreated by the local population. PAA-Africa's air crew members began to carry a letter issued by the British High Command of the East and the U.S. Army Air Corps, printed in both Arabic and English, requesting that assistance be provided to the bearer of the letter. [See Appendix C.]

*A British pilot
demonstrates the
preferred method of
conducting a forced
landing. Note the white
paint on the rear
portion of the fuselage,
used to help rescuers
locate aircraft downed
in the desert.*

Downed aircraft were recovered either by loading them on to trucks and carrying them back to a nearby PAA-Africa base or flying them out to the nearest PAA airfield. Repair work was not too difficult. Aircraft usually needed only a new propeller. The landing gear was lowered by digging sloping ditches under the wings. Only refuelling was needed before takeoff. Major repairs were completed when the aircraft returned to a main PAA-Africa airfield. When a complete recovery of the aircraft was not possible, salvage crews would remove the radios, guns, and other valuable pieces of equipment.

By spring 1942, more of the American-built four-engined bombers were flying on the route. Many of these "Big Boys" encountered problems with navigational mistakes and mechanical failures that forced them down. Several of the bombers ran into problems while crossing the South Atlantic and were in serious trouble by the time they reached the African continent. Several bombers had to attempt landings on the beaches of West Africa when they could not reach Roberts Field. Once an aircraft was overdue, PAA's station managers would use their radio system to notify other aircraft in the area to be on the lookout for the missing aircraft. Paul Mantz, the famous Hollywood stunt pilot and movie man who served as a pilot in the U.S. Army Air Corps, was involved in several recovery attempts of bomber aircraft that had to make forced landings in Liberia.

Africa was rough on the P-40s. An aircraft is seen here being repaired in the bush. This scene was repeated all across Africa as PAA crews were deployed to recover damaged aircraft.

Numerous rescue missions were flown from El Fasher, as the smaller fighter aircraft were often operating near their range limits. If they missed the field, they would have to accomplish a "forced landing" in the bush. Once an entire flight of P-40s missed the field and were lost in the bush for several days. PAA-Africa sent one of its two Grumman amphibians to El Fasher to assist in that search effort.

Captain Steve Shaw, a Grumman G-21A pilot based in Liberia, participated in several rescue missions along the Liberian coast. German submarines, active off the coast of Liberia, torpedoed many ships and Captain Shaw dropped supplies to the shipwrecked sailors in their lifeboats. His efforts accounted for numerous "saves." After Shaw left Liberia, David Farabough took over and continued to add to the total of rescued seaman.

On 29 June 1942, Eddy Frankiewicz and his C-53 crew participated in a rescue mission in central Africa. The station manager at El Fasher notified him that a U.S. Army Air Corps B-24 bomber was down in the area and asked for a search. They found the aircraft and saw that it appeared to be in good condition. The B-24 bomber had made a gear-down landing and was flyable. Upon landing, the rescue crew found that a U.S. Air Corps Brigadier General (Hadley) and a Royal Air Force Air Vice Marshal (Forbes) were on board. Neither was particularly happy. A decision was reached to return the VIP passengers to El Fasher on the C-53 before transporting fuel to the site and attempting to relaunch the B-24.

The actual rescue of Canadian merchant seamen who survived the sinking of their ship by a German U-Boat. Pan Am's Grumman aircraft were used for many such operations along the West African coast.

Tin Can Wealth

Returning from El Fasher, the C-53 carried 60 five-gallon shiny tin cans of aviation gasoline. Both crews started to unload the 30-lb. cans and laboriously manhandled the first cans, via the bomb bay, through the upper fuselage hatch, onto the wing of the B-24. Using the pointed end of a crash ax, holes were punched in the can and the contents emptied into the wing tank of the aircraft. The first empty can was tossed down and offered to a 6'8" tall, regal-looking local Chief, who had been observing the operation. He smiled at the gift, uttered a few words, and made a few gestures. Thirty equally tall natives immediately appeared and started to make easy work of carrying the remaining fuel cans to the wing in the more than 100°F temperature. The Chief became a wealthy man that day, the proud owner of 60 empty five-gallon shiny tin cans. In Africa, any type of container to carry water, or any other equally necessary commodity, is a valuable asset.

Another unusual rescue started on 11 July 1942, PAA-Africa's Senior Pilot, Captain Henry C. Kristofferson, and his crew were at El Geneina, in western Sudan, when they heard that another PAA-Africa C-47, piloted by Captain J. A. Worrell, was reported down somewhere southwest of the field. Loaded with a doctor, spare parts, and a crew to fix the broken aircraft, they left El Geneina and initiated an airborne search. Carl Antone, radio operator on Kristofferson's crew, was able to talk to the downed crew and took a radio bearing to guide the rescue plane to the scene, which was near the village of Goz Beida. Local Africans, who had come on the scene of the downed aircraft, quickly cleared some bush and made a temporary landing site. Their clearing was short and Capt. Kristofferson had everyone on board his aircraft move to the back before landing. During the landing roll-out, the right gear dropped into some mud and the aircraft ground looped. With the help of about 60 Africans, the aircraft was pulled out of the mud with ropes attached to each landing-gear strut. The landing strip was then lengthened and the rescue aircraft, now loaded with the crew of the downed aircraft and their cargo, took-off and returned to El Geneina. A repair crew was sent to the site and established its own "Bush City," and began to repair the downed aircraft. The urgency of the work increased significantly when the repair crew noticed that the water level of a nearby river was rising rapidly. The repairs were completed and the aircraft moved away from the river bed before the area near Bush City was inundated. After four weeks the damaged aircraft was flown back to Accra.

Maiduguri, Nigeria, also had its share of air crew rescue missions, such as when Milo Bacon and Dwight Shrum were passing through on a west-bound DC-3 flight. They heard that a U.S. Army Lockheed was down near Maiduguri. Milo and Dwight had Air Vice Marshal Lloyd of the R.A.F. with them as a passenger. As the Americans prepared to launch their search mission, Lloyd volunteered to go along and assist, stating that an extra pair of eyes was always useful in a search operation. They finally located the downed pilots and dropped a note telling them that help would soon be on the way. This episode was just another occasion when different organizations in Africa pitched in to help each other.

Sadly, some of the rescue missions were not successful. Serious accidents did happen, and men died in Africa. In a memorandum to Harold Bixby dated 20 March 1942, Frank Gledhill told of some of the tragedies.

The PAA C-47 destroyed on the ground at Khartoum. The landing gear strut exploded during servicing.

(Top) The local population was very interested in the big bird that landed near their homes. (Middle) The aircraft came to rest pointed directly at the nearby river, which can be seen in the background. (Bottom) Hand-drilling under the wing to repair damage.

(Top) Duct Tape: a maintenance man's most important tool.
(Middle) The dress code suggests that lunch was an informal
affair at Bush City. (Bottom) The work crew at Bush City.

1. Pilot Day, working for the British getting P-40s from Port
Sudan to Cairo is lost. No trace of him and the search has been
abandoned.

2. An undercarriage caved in at Fasher and injured some people under the wing. The airplane has been flown back to Accra for
repairs.

3. A CO_2 (carbon dioxide) bottle being used to inflate a shock
strut on a C-53 exploded while the plane was being serviced at
Khartoum. Killed the Chief Mechanic (Arthur C. Gordon) burned
two other PAA personnel, one seriously. Dr. Yeomans has been in
attendance and Dr. Coggeshall visited the boys tonight. As a result of the explosion the plane caught fire.

The second mechanic involved in the Khartoum accident, Earle E. Crooks,
died from his injuries several days later. Both men were buried at Khartoum.
On 23 May 1942, a PAA-Africa transport plane crashed in Freetown, Sierra
Leone, killing 23 passengers and crew.

PAA-Africa's Personnel Manager, Voit Gilmore, reported that ten
employees died in Africa, out of a total population of more than 1,300. They
were buried in grave sites at Freetown, Takoradi, Lagos, Oshogbo, Khartoum,
and Port Sudan. Not all of the crash victims were recovered. One downed

*American victims of an airplane crash in Nigeria are laid to rest during a funeral
ceremony in the European Cemetery in Oshogbo on 12 April 1942. Fatalities
included: Captain Frank Cordova–PAA, Ralph Murry–PAA, 2nd Lt. D. R. Whipple–
Air Corps, and Master Sgt. H. M. Kent–Air Corps. Seen standing at the foot of the
coffins are Captain S. L. Gumport–PAA, M.C. Gravis–PAA, Lt. L. Milch–Air Corps,
and Captain F.P. Glen,–PAA. Reverend Littleton (far right), from the Baptist
College in Iwo, Nigeria, officiated at the ceremony. (National Archives)*

P-40 ferry pilot wrote a note on his aircraft's wing telling would-be rescuers that he was walking. His note included an arrow showing the direction. He had broken the golden rule that a pilot should always stay with the aircraft. He was never found.

Radio Operators

Roland Fife, as Division Communications Superintendent, was responsible for setting up the radio system in Africa. The first PAA-Africa-installed radio station was completed in Accra on 14 November 1941 and used the call sign "BOZ 2." Thirteen ground stations were constructed along the route: Maiduguri, Lagos, and Kano in Nigeria; Khartoum, El Fasher, and El Geneina in Anglo-Egyptian Sudan; Freetown in Sierra Leone; Roberts Field and Fisherman's Lake in Liberia; Fort Lamy in French Equatorial Africa; Salalah in the Sultanate of Oman; and Gura in Eritrea.

PAA-Africa's radio operators, working from ground stations and from aircraft, were vital to the success of the mission. As the third member of the DC-3 air crew, the radio operator provided a vital link between the aircraft and the headquarters in Accra. He had to send and receive coded messages and maintain "listening watch" on the emergency frequency, 500 kilocycles, often spending many hours airborne with little to occupy his time.

Some radio operators used SCR 274 Liaison Radios, that were installed in the aircraft to practice their "ham" radio skills. Using their personal call signs and jargon, they could shoot the breeze with their friends and colleagues from Liberia to Cairo. PAA-Africa received word that the British were very concerned about the strange transmissions near 2 megacycles frequency, and the practice was stopped.

Flying Lesson

As the third crew member, many radio operators could obtain some "Stick Time" flying the aircraft. During one such flight, Carl Antone was invited to sit in the pilot's seat. He received some basic flying instruction from the co-pilot who then excused himself to go back to the lavatory. Antone was flying the aircraft like a pro until he noticed the nose was going up. He applied the correction, but then the nose dipped too far down. Another correction and the nose went up. This went on for some time. He then looked back, to see that the two pilots were running back and forth through the cabin, making the aircraft pitch up and down.

Ground Operations

PAA-Africa's Construction Division designed and built many installations during its short tenure in Africa. The effort was led by a team of engineers working at their drafting tables in New York City. The construction team in the field consisted of more than 400 men, skilled as carpenters, electricians, bridgemen, steel foremen, diesel mechanics, glazers, painters, plumbers, embarkation clerks, tractor operators, refrigeration experts, and iron workers. Employees assigned to the Construction Department, as a group, were the oldest Americans working for PAA in Africa. Their average age was 36.

The list of the different types of structures built by the Construction Department is long. An internal corporate memorandum dated 30 November 1943, from Construction Manager Willis C. Lowe, titled Revised List of Buildings, demonstrates the massive scope of the construction projects undertaken in Africa by PAA-Africa, Ltd.

Acetylene Generator Buildings	Fire Equipment Buildings	Office Buildings
Administration Buildings	Finance Buildings	Parachute Shops
Barber Shops	Garages	Paint Shops
Battery Shops	Guard Houses	Pump Houses
Butcher Shops	Hospital	Power Houses
Carpenter Shops	Hangars with Shops Attached	Pantries
Cadmium Plating Shops	Headquarters Buildings	Police Posts
Cafeteria Buildings	Hydrogen Generator Buildings	Plumbing Shops
Chemical Laboratories	Inflammable Storage Buildings	Radio Shops
Classrooms	Kitchens	Radio Transmission Receiving Buildings
Cold Storage Buildings	Lumber Storage Buildings	Radio Masts
Commissary Storehouses	Link Trainer Buildings	Stockrooms
Churches	Laundries	Slaughter-Houses
Compressor House	Mechanical Shops	Staff Buildings
Dining Halls	Medical Inspections Buildings	Staff Quarters
Dormitories	Native Barracks	Shower Buildings
Dope Shops	Native Kitchens	Toilet and Locker Rooms
Direction Finder Stations	Native Laundries	Testing Laboratories
Engine Overhaul Buildings	Native Toilets and Showers	Warehouses
Engine Storage Buildings	Oil Storage Buildings	Water Towers
Engine Test Buildings		Water Tanks
Electric Shops		Wells

Buildings in the western part of the route, where heavy rains occurred, were usually built with hollow cement blocks. Those in the dryer desert locations were constructed with solid sun-dried mud bricks. Floors of all structures were solid concrete slabs raised 12" to 18" above ground level. Mosquito screens were used on all living areas. Electricity was installed in all buildings and eventually modern plumbing with toilets, wash basins, and showers were installed. At some of the stations that had severe water shortages, "honey buckets" had to substitute for flush toilets. These PAA buildings were transferred to the U.S. Army when the military took control of the operation in December 1942.

Medical Services

The senior medical officer for PAA in Africa was Dr. Chester Coggeshall. He had a staff of seven other doctors, a dentist, male nurses, laboratory diagnosticians, and medical entomologists. The biggest challenge was malaria. At the time of their arrival in the Gold Coast in 1941, the colony was known to have an almost 100 percent malarial infection rate. At that time, white men were particularly susceptible to the strain of this disease which was carried by the mosquito anapheles gambiae.

Applying and adapting procedures first tested in Central and Latin America, the PAA medical staff oversaw a wide ranging effort to reduce the impact of the disease. Mosquito breeding areas were drained, ditches dug and oiled, barracks were given double layers of screens, and sprayed daily in an attempt to halt the spread of malaria. Most employees took daily doses of quinine or atabrine. Additionally, high-topped mosquito boots and long trousers became the standard dress code from sundown to bedtime.

A group of PAA fellows relaxing in their barracks. The mosquito netting on the bunks (and the cigar) discouraged the insects. The gin was, of course, for medicinal purposes.

A typical civilian pilot's uniform issued in Accra, included a side arm and mosquito boots, as modelled here by youthful Pilot Harry Jenkins in 1942.

Finger-tip blood samples were drawn from the pilots and tested for malaria before their missions. By the end of 1942, the medical team had lowered the incidence rate for malaria among PAA's staff from 30 – 40 percent to about 1 percent.

Dysentery was the next most serious problem facing the company's staff along the air route. The problem was ameliorated as the medical department instituted strict sanitation standards at all the stations along the route.

Meteorology

In 1941, Pan American Airways Atlantic Division's Meteorologist Tom Hoopes, a Pan Am weather specialist, prepared a summary of surface and upper air data from all African observing stations. After completing the task, Tom accepted a position as the assistant to George Matrisciana, who served as the senior Meteorologist for PAA-Africa. Much of the preparation and training for the other meteorology specialists, hired to work in Africa, was accomplished on the journey to Africa on board the *S.S. Acadia*.

The first group of meteorologists worked 12-hour days during the first months in Africa. They had the Forecast Office operational in about ten days. Many of these men contracted malaria, but they continued to work through the fever.

The major weather problems faced by PAA-Africa included the Harmattan dust and haze, Sudan's haboob sandstorms, ground fog in Liberia, and West African tornadoes, which were lines of thunderstorms that would eventually turn into full hurricanes, once they moved off the coast of West Africa.

The airport weather station and light
beacon tower at Roberts Field, Liberia.

Commissary

Kevin Howard, who was recruited from
the Hotel Management School at Cornell
University, served as the Superintendent of
the Commissary Department. He hired
several others with training at Cornell,
including Jack Kersey, who became the
Port Steward in Accra.

Maintenance

James Weesner, PAA-Africa's Maintenance Superintendent, was stationed at
Accra. His department boasted the largest number of employees in Africa, as
well as the youngest, with an average age of only 22. The PAA-Africa story
evolves around the maintenance crews and their ability to keep the aircraft
operating along the air route. For example, in Kano, the large B-17 bombers
had to be refueled by a hand pump out of 55-gallon barrels. The maintenance
crew jury-rigged a motorized pump to speed up the process. Eventually, a
4,000-gallon tank truck was delivered to Kano and this solved the problem,
but in the meantime the ingenuity of the maintenance crews sped up B-17
deliveries to the Pacific region.

Maintenance shifts were established to accommodate the local environment. In Accra, during the early days of the operation, most of the work was
done during the daylight hours. The risk of malaria was too high to authorize
outdoor evening activities. On the other hand, in Khartoum, all maintenance
was accomplished at night, because the daylight temperatures were too hot
for working outside, and the malaria threat was much less in Khartoum than
Accra. Many of the men preferred to work in Khartoum, with the more interesting unannounced arrivals of aircraft coming in to the station from all four
cardinal directions. A radio silence policy provided little advanced warning of
an incoming flight. Compared to the activity level in Khartoum, Accra was
considered to be somewhat boring.

The Africans

PAA-Africa, and later the U.S. Army, were dependent upon the help of the local Africans to accomplish many of the tasks involved in building and maintaining the air route. PAA-Africa hired more than 1,500 Africans at the main operating base in Accra alone. The jobs varied greatly. At Accra, the meteorology office hired two Africans as map plotters. They helped to produce map products covering the weather situation from Dakar to Cairo. Others worked in various skilled and non-skilled positions. In his *African Report,* Voit Gilmore wrote about the relationships between the Americans and the Africans. He stated that:

> In addition to the official relationship between the company and its native personnel, there developed a feeling of friendship and mutual admiration among the Americans and their native associates which certainly can be counted one of the most outstanding phases of the Trans-African operation. Without the direct, solicitous approach of missionaries, Pan American brought to thousands of natives throughout its route a realistic interpretation of the American way of living and a graphic lesson in American standards for business and social conduct.

As the U.S. Army took control of the airfield in Accra, the number of employed native personnel increased to more than 7,000 by July 1943. The higher-skilled workers were used as draftsmen, surveyors, clerks, carpenters, electricians, plumbers, blacksmiths, powerhouse operators, and painters. Unskilled work included sanitation chores and other common labor. Additionally, the U.S. Army established a Native Guard unit to police the base. The Africans were paid at governmental wage scale, which was slightly higher than the average wages being paid in the colony. Some Africans traveled hundreds of miles to work in Accra.

Many local African employees still recall those years. One group formed a Ghana-U.S. Veterans Association, remembering their days working for the Americans in Accra.

Free Time

Long working hours and incomplete camp structures did not leave much free time for the first employees—the PAA-Africa "trailblazers"—arriving in Africa. As construction was completed, and larger numbers of staff arrived, there was more leisure time.

In Accra, the seashore was the major recreational site. Teshi Beach, claimed by many to rival Waikiki, offered an excellent palm tree-lined beach and a great place to "get away from it all." Swimming was problematic, as the ocean tides and currents were dangerous. Small surfboards were available for the 1940s version of body-surfing.

Golf and tennis were available in the city of Accra. The golf course had sand "browns" instead of grass "greens." The "browns" were the normal "greens" made out of sand. The tennis courts were made of clay; players could hire a local ball boy at a nickel for the entire afternoon.

Athletic fields were provided for staff at the PAA Camp in Accra. There was a baseball diamond, horseshoes, tennis courts, volleyball, badminton, handball courts, and even a regulation-size basketball court. The men could rent bicycles on their days off and visit the local community. Roy Moungovan managed to purchase an English moped which he could use to tow several friends on rented bicycles around the countryside. Others purchased and rebuilt old German, Italian, and English motorcycles.

Heavenly Design
Father Harold Rigney, a Catholic chaplain from Chicago, supplemented his mission work in the Gold Coast by coming to PAA's Accra camp every Sunday to celebrate Mass in the recreation hall. After several months, a group of the routine attendees finally determined that they needed a real chapel for Father Rigney.

This idea caught the imagination of Assistant Manager John Yeomans, who gave informal encouragement to the Catholics, non-Catholics, Americans, and Africans willing to contribute their time to design and build a chapel. Several unused shower houses, measuring 18 x 24 feet, were used for the construction project. Partitions were removed and corners trimmed as the showers were transformed into a chapel.

The chapel in Accra, Gold Coast. The sign on the left welcomes both Catholics and Protestants to worship under the same roof.

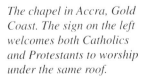

Using local unpolished mahogany wood, native cabinet makers carved a confessional, cross, pulpit, thirty-two pews, and other artistic trim items. A steeple and belfry soon sprouted from the structure. Supplies and equipment began to appear miraculously. Brigadier General Fitzgerald, the senior U.S. Army officer at Accra, unknowingly donated the reddish-brown drapes from his DC-3 which were made into curtains for the altar. An organ and stained glass windows were obtained locally. The church bell was borrowed from an old locomotive located in the Accra railroad yards.

As the project was nearing completion, Captain Cyril Goyette took Father Rigney for his first flight to have an "angel's eye" view of the chapel, which was dedicated to St. Joseph of Cupertino, the patron of aviators.

After the dedication, the builders also offered their chapel to Father Wallace Wolverton, the Episcopalian Minister. He used it to conduct Protestant services for the men of PAA-Africa.

In Liberia, the beaches were again a major draw for the PAA staff. Additionally, the U.S. Army engineers, who arrived in May and June 1942, had a band, which gave periodic concerts. Many of their musicians were army volunteers who had been playing with some of the well-known swing bands in the United States, such as Duke Ellington, Count Basie, Jimmy Lunceford, and Chick Webb. According to the PAA-Africa pilots who attended the concerts, they were world-class musical performances.

The U.S. Army Engineers brought their band with them to Liberia. Here they parade for the local population. The band performed frequently before U.S. and Liberian audiences. (National Archives)

In the Gold Coast and Liberia, some of the staff would travel into the African bush to visit the home villages of Africans who were working at the airfields. Many Americans wanted to visit the "real" Africa to witness ceremonial events and to photograph the natural beauty of the bush. The company allowed the men to use the camp buses for these outings. In Sudan and Nigeria, hunting was a major way to pass the time and to supplement the dinner table.

The company also established a "Flying Library" for its employees in Africa, with 1,100 books providing a cross-section of different types of literature. The Library was based in Accra and books were circulated by aircraft between the different operating sites.

Some of the PAA pilots just could not get enough flying. Bart Hewitt and Edward Frankiewicz managed to do some "sport flying" while in Cairo, renting a de Havilland Gypsy Moth biplane for sight-seeing.

What Was the Real Mission?

Many of the flight and ground staff managers in Africa were constantly bewildered and stymied, trying to define their real mission and the priority they should place on different tasks on any particular day. Their assignments often changed as the war progressed. Contradictory directives were sometimes received from different agencies and governments. These included the U.S. Army, which had liaison officers assigned at most operating locations; the British Government; and PAA-Africa's headquarters in New York. Sometimes the mission and priorities changed on a daily basis.

The U.S. Consul in Lagos, Nigeria, Perry N. Jester, perhaps described it best in his 18 December 1941 memorandum to the Department of State in Washington, D.C. In explaining the situation of PAA-Africa, Ltd. in Lagos, he stated that,

> The whole organization of this company out here is still in the throes of settling in and consequently it is too early to report effectively on what the final dispositions of their personnel and of their services will be. Their original plans in many respects have already undergone certain changes and I believe that even further changes will be made, hence I have been waiting until their organization has become more settled before attempting to report on this subject.

As the U.S. involvement in the war increased, so did the number of modifications to the tasks performed by PAA-Africa. The situation never stabilized.

Altering the Course
of the War

J udging the immediate impact of any one military unit on the wartime efforts of a nation is difficult at best. But, in the case of PAA-Africa, Ltd., this one non-military, corporate unit provided immeasurable assistance to the fighting forces of the United Kingdom, the United States, and eventually many of the other Allied nations fighting against the Axis powers. PAA-Africa played a part in altering the balance of power in many battles, and contributed to the outcome of the entire conflict. The list of diverse activities and missions that PAA-Africa supported is long. It includes many episodes of courage under fire, as well as dangerous exploits to save the lives of wounded soldiers and to deliver critically needed war supplies, so that the battles against the Axis powers could continue. All these events occurred in a rather short period, as PAA-Africa's operational activities in Africa were condensed into a mere fourteen months.

The Aerial Burma Road 1942

One of the most significant flight operations that occurred during the short operational lifetime of PAA-Africa was its participation in the India-Burma-China resupply mission. These missions in the Far East were conducted as a joint operation with units from PAA-Africa, Ltd. joining with the U.S. Army's 10th Air Ferry Command. Additionally, the China National Airline Corporation (C.N.A.C.) and the R.A.F. provided aircraft and air crews.

By March 1942, the situation in Burma was being watched closely in Washington and London. The Burma Road had been severed as the Japanese Army advanced rapidly into Burma. The Road was the only practical ground route to supply the forces of Generalissimo Chiang Kai-shek and his Chinese Nationalist government, who were doing battle with the Japanese in China. During a 3 March 1942 meeting of the United States/British Combined Chiefs of Staff, held in room #240 of the Public Health Service Building in Washington, D.C., General "Hap" Arnold explained to his British counterparts that 38 transport aircraft were operating between Takoradi and Calcutta.

He stated that the intent of the United States was to increase this number to
138 transport aircraft. These aircraft would be used mainly for building up
U.S. forces operating in India and Burma. On 7 March 1942, the British evacuated Rangoon in the face of the advancing Japanese. The military situation
in Burma became critical as the threat to the heart of India was real, and no
time could be wasted for the planned increase in the transport aircraft fleet.

The U.S. Army's 10th Ferry Command, operating out of bases in India,
was assigned the original mission of providing the emergency airlift support.
The first priority was to deliver 30,000 gallons of 100 octane aviation fuel and
a quantity of .50 caliber ammunition to Loi Wing, China. The cargo was
destined for the P-40s of Claire Chenault's American Volunteer Group
(A.V.G.). Colonel Caleb V. Haynes was in command of the small group of
U.S. transport aircraft and the military and civilian volunteer air crews
carrying this high priority cargo into China. Although this mission has been
reported to be an all-volunteer operation, the initial directive to PAA-Africa,
to send ten of their transport aircraft to India, was anything but a request. On
25 March 1942, Headquarters, Army Air Forces Ferry Command, Washington, D.C., sent the following memorandum to PAA Headquarters:

INDIA-CHINA AIR ROUTE
("THE HUMP")

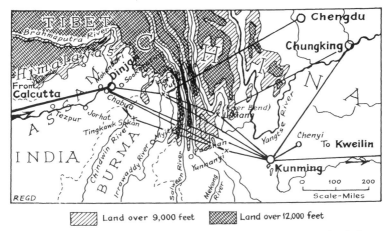

*The eastern terminus of the PAA-Africa network was Dinjan, in the Indian
province, Assam. During the first few months of 1942, this was the base for the
celebrated "Hump" pilots, who braved the precipitous mountain ridges of
southwest China to supply the Chinese bases at Kumming, Chungking, and
Chengtu, and to evacuate troops and refugees.*

You are instructed to move ten DC type aircraft off the African Run
immediately to General Brereton at New Delhi on temporary loan
until project is completed and then return to the African Run.

Paul Bird, Jr.
1st Lt., Air Corps
Assistant S-3

In Accra, PAA-Africa's staff immediately identified the ten aircraft that
would go to India and issued a call for volunteer pilots and crew to fly the
missions. On 9 April 1942, the aircraft and the crews started to leave Accra
for the long journey to India. The PAA-Africa civilian crews were absorbed
into the U.S. Army's flight operations. The combined U.S. Army and PAA-
Africa aircraft and crews were supplemented by other PAA-Africa aircraft
and personnel who also participated at irregular intervals.

American transport aircraft activities were based at Dinjan Airport in
India. The airfield was home to a mixed group of occupants, including the
U.S. Army/PAA-Africa transport group, R.A.F. fighters and transports,
C.N.A.C., A.V.G., and other Chinese air units. Subject to daylight bombing
raids by the Japanese, Dinjan was used only at night. During the day, most of
the aircraft were away from the field flying missions or dispersed to outlying
airfields.

The original mission assigned to the PAA-Africa crews was to transport
30,000 gallons of aviation fuel from Calcutta's Dum Dum Airfield to Dinjan.
This was quickly accomplished. Next, PAA crews were tasked to airlift the
fuel to China, carrying it as cargo in 5-gallon cans and also tankered in one of
the internal fuel tanks of the aircraft. 100 octane fuel was used by the transport
aircraft for takeoffs and landings, but the rest of the flight was flown using 90
octane fuel from the other tanks on the aircraft. Additional airlift requirements
surfaced as the Japanese Imperial Army continued to advance into Burma.

*Captains Ziegler and
Eveland (PAA-Africa)
oversee the off-loading
of their precious
cargo—civilian
refugees fleeing from
the Japanese Army in
Burma. The
photograph was taken
at Dinjan, India, in
April 1942.*

*PAA crews shared the airfield at Loi Wing, China, with the men of the A.V.G.
Flying Tigers. This was one of their Curtiss P-40s.*

*The mess hall of a nearby tea plantation served as the living quarters for the PAA
crews while they operated out of Dinjan in April 1942.*

The "Hump" was an understated description of the terrain between Assam and southwestern China. Successive ranges of mountains, separated by deep chasms (formed by the Irrawaddy, Salween, Mekong, and Yangtse rivers), were more precipitous than the Rocky Mountains, and created serious meteorological problems for the air crews. A forced landing was almost certainly fatal.

R.A.F. and U.S. Army personnel, ammunition, weapons, P-40 spare parts, and foodstuffs were all part of the cargoes transported by PAA-Africa's air crews to China.

Colonel Haynes's small group of transport aircraft became the real pioneers of flying "the Hump," as this hazardous route across the eastern Himalayas was soon called. These men operated in the most geographically hostile environment on earth. Their aircraft had no supplemental oxygen systems, but the crews had to fly high over the mountains. They had inaccurate aerial charts. The base at Dinjan was not even on some of the maps. Most of the radio aids for navigation were shut down for fear of providing Japanese aircraft with navigational assistance, and there were no weather reports. The PAA DC-3s did not have de-icing boots nor any alcohol to de-ice the cockpit windows or propeller blades, even though they routinely had to fly at altitudes of 16,000 feet or higher to cross the "Hump."

The mission soon changed to include the delivery of 37mm ammunition to the British forces under attack at Lashio. The crews quickly loaded the cargo and delivered it to Lashio, only to be told upon landing that there was not a 37mm gun within 100 miles and that what the troops really needed was standard .303 rifle ammunition.

As the transport air crews moved east into Burma, they routinely operated from airfields at Lashio and Myitkyina (pronounced 'Mitch-E-naw'). In China they used the airfields at Loi Wing and Kunming. Lashio fell to the Japanese on 30 April 1942.

Crisis at Myitkyina

Mission requirements constantly changed. By the last week in April, the American air crews on their return flights to Dinjan were directed to evacuate British Army forces and civilian refugees from Myitkyina. After delivering cargo to airfields in China and Burma, they would stop at Myitkyina's isolated 3,000-foot gravel landing strip at the northern terminus of the Burma railroad, which was flooded with refugees fleeing from the rapidly advancing Japanese. Pandemonium often broke out on the airstrip. Refugees would rush the aircraft as they landed and try to force their way on board. Crews were forced to rev-up the port engines and literally blow the crowds away from the aircraft's door. The refugees that could not be taken out by air knew that their only alternative would be to walk out of Burma over the treacherous mountain trails to India. This would mean certain death, except for those most physically fit. Don Stoeger made his first run into Burma on 17 April 1942; he picked up 52 refugees and logged 2 hours, 15 minutes on the flight from Myit-

"Operations Shack" at Loi Wing, China. "Olson & Co. Exterminators... 24 Hr. Service." Commanding Officer of the 3rd A.V.G. Squadron was Arvid Olson, a classmate of PAA's Captain Eveland, Class 40-B, Kelly AFB.

kyina to Dinjan. There were many heartrending scenes as families were broken up. Seriously injured and dying stretcher cases relinquished their place on the aircraft to the younger soldiers so that they might be saved to continue the fight against the Japanese. Try as they would, the pilots were not able to get all the wounded soldiers and refugees out of Myitkyina by air. Besides wounded British and Indian troops, the evacuees included British and American journalists, and family members of employees of Standard Oil, Coca Cola, Kodak, and the Burma Oil Company.

The final day of flight operations into Myitkyina began routinely on 6 May 1942, with a PAA-Africa crew, Wayne Eveland and Leo Viens, waiting for orders to depart Dinjan. But on this day, the PAA crew received a message to return to the Operations Building. Two R.A.F. transports were observed taking off. It was later learned that Dallas B. Sherman, PAA-Africa's chief pilot in Dinjan, told Col. Haynes that PAA's crews would not fly unless there was positive word that the airfield at Myitkyina was still in the hands of friendly forces. An animated dispute broke out between Sherman and Col. Haynes. The protracted and heated discussion ended later that day when reports were received that the two R.A.F. transport planes, which had departed earlier that morning bound for Myitkyina, had been destroyed by the Japanese as they landed there. There were no more evacuation flights to Myitkyina. Radio reports from the Burma underground confirmed that there was wholesale slaughter of the remaining refugees by the Japanese. All of the horrors of war converged at this one small airstrip in Burma. But the lives of more than 3,000 soldiers and refugees were saved, and the lives of these ten PAA-Africa air crews would never be the same again.

Working in the war zone created many difficult operational control and legal issues for the civilian air crews. Operational imperatives and lack of sufficient personnel support meant that few records were made of these activities. To exacerbate the situation, PAA's crews could not make contact with their superiors back in Accra because of the secrecy surrounding the operation. Flights were routinely made over enemy-held territory and in airspace where the Japanese had gained air superiority. The American transport aircraft were unarmed and pursuit protection from friendly fighter aircraft was negligible.

PAA-Africa's Chief Pilot, Dallas B. Sherman, wrote about the events in his after-action report, titled: Observations of Joint Operations PAA-Africa, Ltd. and U.S. Army, Assam Burma-China Ferry Command, Dinjan, India; April 5th to May 15th, 1942. Sherman stated that:

> In addition to the possibility of enemy occupation of territory, it was established that much of the remote regions in the supposedly friendly territory was inhabited by "head hunters" and other unfriendly Burmese or Chinese tribes. The use of parachutes by crew members was out of the question on most flights due to the presence of passengers for which parachutes were not provided. Advance weather reports were inadequate or lacking entirely. Guards, with instructions to shoot, were employed on each flight carrying refugees or soldiers, because of possible fifth column presence. Many of the wounded, sick or refugees had diseases of questionable contagion. Vomiting and other sicknesses aboard the aircraft was the normal reaction of the refugees due to fright, fatigue, inadequate or improper food. The stench of gangrene was noticeable in most of the cabins. No adequate methods of cabin fumigation or sanitation were available. At each airport from which evacuees were removed the control progressed steadily from bad to worse. Loading went from weighed and listed passengers to wild mobs pushing their way aboard in uncertain numbers and weight. There was one instance of a man forcing his way aboard with a gun. He was later removed by gun threat before takeoff. Many injustices were done in rejection of certain refugees and in the acceptance aboard of others, but this was to a large degree unavoidable under the circumstances.

During this operation 3,564 evacuees were carried out of Burma. One PAA-Africa evacuation mission carried a total of 71 passengers and 3 crew members in a single DC-3 aircraft. The normal authorized load of a DC-3 was only 28 passengers plus 3 crew members. PAA-Africa pilot Don Stoeger, recalling the events of 1942, stated that:

> Because of the imminent danger to the fleeing civilians and soldiers, U.S. pilots were quickly influenced to add progressively to the number of passengers loaded irrespective of aircraft CG loading and maximum gross weight limitations from short-field situations. Pilots were fully aware of the fact that the extreme aft center of gravity of the aircraft caused by the excessive overloading was way beyond any reasonable limits and presented an exceedingly dangerous flight condition. In the face of the advancing enemy troops, each flight became more of a desperate attempt by skilled and responsible pilots to help these unfortunate people without killing them, or ourselves, in the process.

The horizontal stabilizer of one PAA-Africa C-47 was severely damaged during a Japanese air attack against Loi Wing on 28 April 1942. Capt. Wayne Eveland and his First Officer, Millard Nasholds, are wondering, "What do we do now?"

During all of these operations between India, Burma, and China, only one PAA-Africa Ltd. aircraft was damaged because of hostile action. On 28 April 1942, a DC-3, piloted by Wayne Eveland, was caught on the ground during a 24-plane Japanese bombing raid at Loi Wing, China. The aircraft suffered significant bomb damage with the loss of a major section of its horizontal tail assembly. Five other PAA-Africa aircraft escaped damage. One of the PAA-Aircraft, piloted by Don Stoeger, managed to get airborne and escaped as the Japanese bombs were falling. The next day a replacement left horizontal stabilizer was flown-in from Dinjan and Eveland's aircraft was repaired and back in the air the next morning.

The return trip, with more than 40 wounded on board, was itself a noteworthy flight for Eveland in his recently repaired aircraft. Beset by monsoon rains he had to divert twice into an airfield in Burma before finally landing in a blinding rain-storm at Dinjan.

PAA-Africa flight crews participating in the Burma evacuation flights from Myitkyina airfield included:

Captains:	*First Officers:*	*Flight Engineers:*
Dallas Sherman	Samual Belieff	Richard O'Keefe
Robert Carstensen	Charles Hammell	Joseph Patrick
Wayne Eveland	Charles McClelland	
Grover Furr	Millard K. Nasholds	
John Heninger	Raymond Sylvester	*Radio Operators:*
James Hubbard	Leo Viens	Peter Kravchenok
Vernon Kerns	Doron Warren	Arthur White
George Lanning	William Zeng	Jack Winn
Victor Looney		
John Ohlinger		
John Passage		
Donald Stoeger		
Jean Ziegler		

Two other PAA-Africa aircraft attempted to participate in India-Burma-China missions but were lost in bad weather en route from Calcutta to Dinjan. Both crews survived their forced landings, but they never made it to Burma to participate in the resupply and evacuation missions. Both aircraft were eventually recovered, repaired, and returned to service on the Africa route.

PAA-Africa's Senior Pilot Sherman listed some of the cargo carried during the six weeks in which PAA crews worked in Asia. The following list of items was taken from the report of the Commanding Officer, Assam Burma-China Ferry Command, to 10th Air Force Headquarters reporting on the work accomplished by the crews from PAA-Africa:

*Wounded British
soldiers on stretchers
are placed in the shade
of the wing while
awaiting evacuation
from Myitkyina to
Dinjan in April 1942.*

Loads Carried Included:
30,000 gallons 100 octane gasoline
500 gallons oil
20 Bren Guns
525,000 rounds Bren Gun ammunition
450,415 rounds .30 ammunition
.50 caliber ammunition to Loi Wing, China
12 U.S. Army Signal Corps men and 3,000 lb. equipment
4 A.V.G. officers and 1,000 lb. equipment
Army jeeps
Ryan airplane and parts
P-40 parts to Kunming
480 wounded British and Indian troops
9 R.A.F. officers and baggage
3,564 evacuees and baggage
1 corpse (evacuee died in flight)
9,420 lb. .50 caliber ammunition and Ethyl gasoline
25 U.S. Army passengers and baggage
3,000 lb. miscellaneous baggage
2,800 lb. foodstuffs

* Numerous miscellaneous flights of administrative, air raid dispersal, "mercy" (medical supplies, food, etc.), or secret missions, were carried out.
* Cholera vaccine was dropped at Kalewa, Burma, during a serious epidemic.

By 16 May 1942, the PAA-Africa aircraft and air crews had left India and returned to Accra. Their mission had come to an end.

Very little formal recognition was given to the PAA-Africa, Ltd. air crew members who participated in this operation. The Chief of Staff of the 10th Air Force sent his personal appreciation for a tough job well done, and the men, who later joined the Army Air Corps, eventually received some belated recognition in the form of the Distinguished Flying Cross (DFC). The award was presented to them a year or so later. These awards were issued with a rather generic citation and all of them read the same:

> (NAME)_____ Air Corps, United States Army. For extraordinary achievement while participating in aerial flights from 1 January 1942 through March 1943. As an air transport command pilot, (NAME)___ flew more than 1,000 hours in pioneering flights incidental to the establishment of air routes across Africa and the Middle East. During this period key personnel and large quantities of vital materiel were transported expeditiously over unmapped terrain where landing facilities and navigational aids were practically nonexistent. Despite the fact that unarmed transport airplanes were on many occasions flown over areas where the risk of enemy interference was ever-present, the entire assignment was completed without accident or injury.

More recently, several individual medals were awarded by the U.S. military. In 1993, Leo Viens received a Distinguished Flying Cross for his heroic actions on 22 April 1942. This award was presented for the evacuation mission on which he carried 74 people out of Burma in a DC-3. In 1996, a Distinguished Flying Cross was awarded posthumously to Donald J. Stoeger, after a persistent 12-year effort by his family to gain the well-deserved recognition. Special Order GB-163, dated 12 March 1996 reads:

> By the direction of the President, Captain Donald J. Stoeger, 0-399831, is awarded the Distinguished Flying Cross for extraordinary achievement from 17 April 1942 to 4 May 1942.
>   By Order of the Secretary of the Air Force

Emergency Airlift of Weapon Fuses to the British

Another significant service provided by crews of PAA-Africa Ltd. was a series of special supply missions to aid the British forces fighting in North

Africa. Their mission was to move critically-needed fuses for anti-tank artillery shells from Lagos, Nigeria, to Cairo.

The date was 3 July 1942. The war was not going well for the British Army in the Western Desert of Egypt. German Field Marshal Erwin Rommel was advancing on Alexandria and Cairo. An emergency message from the British military headquarters went out to Accra at about midnight on 3 July. The British forces of General Montgomery urgently needed special anti-tank artillery fuses and .50 caliber ammunition. Responding to the call for help, six PAA-Africa crews were rousted out of bed and aircraft prepared for immediate departure. The aircraft flew from Accra to Lagos, where other crews stood by to upload the cargo, which had recently arrived in Nigeria by ship. The aircraft were operated continuously through two night-time periods to fly the cargo to Cairo. With night flying in Africa authorized for the first time, the crews changed at Khartoum and the aircraft arrived in Cairo just 33 hours after receipt of the message requesting the urgent support. By the evening of 4 July, the vital fuses were delivered to the British troops and put to use in the Western Desert.

PAA-Africa crew members who participated in this mission included:

Captains:	C. L Hayward	Cotterill
V. L. Kerns	W. B. Townsend	Karstand
S. D. Newell	L. Hill	Carl Antone
C. F. Linenbach	K. F. Ritz	Stempel
L. D. Perry	G.A. Hensler	Peterson
G. C. Furr	C. R. Hammell	Cameron
L. B. Newby	M. Schroeder	
F. B. Lancaster	R. L. Smith	*Flight Mechanics:*
D. B. Dukelow	R. A. Stade	Anderson
E. G. Mathwig		Coulter
Geo. Kraigher	*2nd Officer*	Mead
R. L. Minor	M. Camille	Pendergast
1st Officers:	*Radio Operators:*	*Flight Engineer:*
G. B. Newman	Choinecki	Stephen
L. E. Viens	Oppegard	

Because of a maintenance problem encountered in Khartoum and a delayed takeoff, S. D. (Dean) Newell and Leo E. Viens flew the entire trip from Accra to Cairo. One of the aircraft crashed while making the night takeoff from Khartoum. The crew walked away from the wreck, but the aircraft and its cargo were destroyed.

In addition to PAA-Africa, the U.S. Army Air Corps, operating from the United States, and the R.A.F.'s. Ferry Command, operating from Canada, also carried high-priority cargo to support this mission. Using the trans-Africa route, aircraft flew directly from the Western Hemisphere to the war zone in Egypt. The first aircraft from Canada to reach Cairo arrived on 17 July 1942.

In an official U.S. Army film reenactment of the July 1942 call for emergency assistance, the U.S. Army Air Corps provided the airlift support. They failed to mention that both PAA-Africa and the R.A.F.'s Ferry Command also participated in the missions to fly the urgently needed cargo to Cairo: another example of PAA civilians receiving little recognition for their work in supporting the war effort.

Evacuation from Cairo

PAA-Africa, Ltd. crews were tasked with another evacuation mission in the first days of July 1942. As a German takeover of Cairo appeared imminent, the new PAA-Africa mission was to evacuate the U.S. North Africa Military Mission staff, the American Legation staff, and other civilians from Cairo. During a 48-hour period, 307 evacuees were carried to safe havens in Luxor, Egypt; Gura, Ethiopia; and Khartoum, Sudan. During the same period, PAA-Africa flew 49 R.A.F. ferry pilots from Cairo to Takoradi to expedite the delivery of additional British war planes to the troops fighting in Egypt. PAA-Africa senior staff assured the U.S. North Africa Military Mission in Cairo and the U.S. Army Air Corps' Ferrying Command, in writing, that it was prepared to continue to operate:

> ... to and from Cairo regardless of the military situation unless and until we are specifically ordered to stop them.

PAA-Africa maintained a six-man staff at the Cairo Heliopolis Airport while the rest of the operation was moved to Luxor.

Wheels of Opportunity
During the evacuation of Cairo in July 1942, PAA-Africa kept a six-man staff in Heliopolis even after the other Americans had left

the city. The PAA men noticed that the American Red Cross employees gave the keys to their Ford station wagon to their Egyptian helper as they boarded the evacuation aircraft. The PAA staff
were able to "borrow" the vehicle. The acquisition was a great
benefit to the night life of the layover crews that were still coming
through Cairo, as they needed wheels to visit the night clubs and
hot spots in central Cairo.

The Red Cross employees, having returned to Cairo, realized that
their station wagon was still in town. The PAA staff did return the
vehicle—albeit reluctantly.

Eastbound Cargo

Of the total cargo carried to the East over the trans-Africa air route, PAA-
Africa's contribution was estimated to be 2,239,500 lb. during the 14 months of
flight activity. In addition to the more routine types of wartime cargoes, such as
aircraft spare parts, ammunition, tires, etc., PAA found that, from time to time,
it was carrying some rather unusual cargo to the combat fronts. For example,
one shipment consisted of "Cynogas A" dust destined for General Stilwell's
forces in Asia. His troops used the pesticide to exterminate vermin. Eastbound
cargo included mail and movies for the troops. There were also reports of large
amounts of cash being shipped to various locations in the region.

Westbound Cargo

Raw rubber and latex were two of the more valuable cargoes routinely
brought back to the U.S. on the westbound flights. Tom MacKay recalls a day
early in August 1942 when he flew a mission out of Accra with PAA-Africa
Captain Tom Collins, flying between Roberts Field, located near the Firestone
Plantation, and Benson Field, located near the seaplane base at Fisherman's
Lake. They logged more than ten hours of flight time that day as they flew four
round-trip missions carrying raw rubber for onward shipment by Pan Am
B-314s at Fisherman's Lake. Incomplete records show that more than 54,000
lb. of crude rubber were shipped back to the U.S. from Africa. Rubber was
vital to the war effort. The B-314 Clippers would carry the cargo on the 14-
hour flight from Fisherman's Lake to South America and then C-47s would
carry it north as far as Miami, for trans-shipment to tire factories operating in
different locations throughout the United States. The rubber caused some
very uncomfortable cabin conditions. Crews and passengers did not savor the
smell of the warm moist rubber and latex.

Local employee of the Firestone Rubber Plantation bounces a bale of rubber as he moves it to a Pan American airplane for the trip to the United States. This raw natural rubber was vital to the war effort.

Captured German equipment was also returned to the United States by air using the trans-Africa route. One of PAA's B-314s carried a barrel and the breech of a German Army 88-millimeter anti-tank cannon that had been captured in the Egyptian desert. The weapon was taken to the Aberdeen Proving Grounds in Maryland for testing and exploitation by the U.S. Army, which also asked PAA-Africa to carry as much mica as possible back from India. Mica was shipped in 200-lb. wooden crates and up to 3,000 lb. was carried on individual DC-3 flights.

Mail was also carried on the westbound flights. [See appendix D for samples of First Day Cover Air Mail envelopes.]

Although not documented, PAA-Africa crews recall that at least one shipment of platinum was carried from Iran on a westbound mission.

A notable human cargo carried westward was one of America's first heroes of the Second World War. Col. James H. Doolittle and several members of his "Tokyo Raiders" made their way back to the United States on board PAA-Africa's aircraft. After completing their 16-bomber raid on Tokyo on 18 April, 1942, the survivors traveled through China, westward towards the United States.

PAA crews first observed Col. Doolittle in Burma late in April on one of the C.N.A.C. DC-3s passing through Myitkyina, Burma. Later that month he was a passenger on a westbound PAA-Africa aircraft on the trip through

Africa. By May 1942, he was back in Washington, where he was promoted to Brigadier General and where, on 19 May 1942, President Roosevelt presented him with the Congressional Medal of Honor.

Personal Tire Delivery

In addition to the many official items that were shipped back to the United States, there were, from time-to-time, unofficial items that made it back to family and friends in the United States. Americans of PAA-Africa brought with them their highly developed sense of Yankee ingenuity. One example of this is told by Dean Newell. He recounts that his mother wrote to him in Africa and explained that she was going to have her car put in storage because of the rationing and shortage of tires in her home town of Inverness, Mississippi. Soon after receiving his mother's note, Dean found himself on a trip to Natal, Brazil, where he noticed several tire manufacturing plants in operation, producing tires that would fit on his mother's car. He purchased four new tubes and tires and found a taxi driver who agreed, for a few dollars, to mount the tires on his taxi and drive on them for a day on the streets of Natal. The tires were then removed to become "used tires." Next, Dean found some friendly ferry pilots who were taking a war-weary B-24 back to Utah for some depot maintenance. After some cajoling the crew agreed to take the four tires with them. He put a small amount of air in each of the tubes and tied the bundle of four tires together with rope. The B-24 departed and the crew had no problem passing through customs in the United States, because they were carrying used tires.

The instructions Dean gave to the pilots were very detailed and included a map, indicating where his mother lived. She was in the southern-most house in Inverness, adjacent to Highway 49. There was a 12-acre pasture just south of the house and several pecan trees along the highway. The written instructions read:

> Enter Inverness from the South, flying low over the pasture and the house. Then make a 360 degree left turn. Come in as low as possible over the south pasture fence, open the bomb-bay doors, and as you cross the fence kick the four tires out.

Dean had instructed his mother to listen for a low-flying aircraft and if one passed, she was to go to the pasture and look for the tires.

One day she heard an airplane pass low overhead. She ran outside to see the tires falling from the aircraft. They rolled towards her and came to rest about 100 feet from her backyard gate. The tires fitted her car and served her well through the remainder of the war years.

Roast Locust

Ingenuity was not limited to the Yanks. The local Africans often displayed their own brand. For example, during a departure from El Fasher, a PAA-Africa C-53 aircraft had a hair-raising experience. Just as the gear was being retracted, the aircraft ran in to a large swarm of flying locusts. The pilot's vision was virtually nil as the windshield was obscured by the mess. The engine oil coolers were plugged and the exposed cylinders heads of the R1830-92 radials were impacted with locusts. The pilots managed to land safely back at El Fasher, but only by sticking their heads out the windows to see the airfield. Once on the ground a native work crew made a reasonably quick job of cleaning up the mess. Their reward—freshly roasted locust plucked from the engine cylinders!

Special Missions

The Special Missions assigned to PAA-Africa were many and varied. No two were ever the same. Most were accomplished as special flights under contract to the U.S. or British Governments. Many were classified and their full stories may never be fully revealed. The trans-Africa air route served a safe pathway for many dignitaries, diplomats, and heads of state to travel to and from the United States after many of the former routes had become extremely dangerous or closed completely because of hostile activities in North Africa and the Mediterranean.

Flight to Kuybyshev

In March 1942, PAA-Africa pilots George Kraigher and Dornan Craig were assigned to fly a VIP Special Mission to Kuybyshev, a city on the Volga River, south-east of Moscow, the Soviet capital. U.S. Ambassador Admiral Stanley was returning to his post in the Soviet Capital. Their flight took them through Basra, Teheran, Baku, and Stalingrad en route to Kuybyshev. PAA's physician, Dr. Coggeshall, was also on board just in case he was needed. As it turned out, Dornan Craig came down with dysentery and the doctor was put to work nursing him back to health.

Note: The Soviet name, Kuybyshev, has now been dropped and the city has restored its original name, Samara.

Wendell Willkie

Late in August 1942, Wendell Willkie, the defeated Indiana Republican candidate for President, came through Africa on a secret mission as a Special Representative of President Roosevelt. A U.S. Army Air Corps crew carried the Willkie Mission using a special Consolidated LB-30 (an early version of the B24/C-87 series) christened *Gulliver*. During a stop in Accra, Willkie gave a pep talk to the PAA personnel. He took the opportunity to lobby the PAA-Africa employees to consider accepting commissions in the U.S. Army and to stay in Africa after the route was fully militarized.

Special Paint Job

On 4 September, with the Willkie party now in Cairo, the American Legation in Cairo notified H. Watson Starcher, the PAA-Africa Acting Special Representative in Egypt, that the Willkie party could not proceed to Turkey as planned on Monday, 7 September. The Turks were insistent that the military B-24-type aircraft would not be allowed to enter their airspace and thus violate Turkish neutrality. They had recently seized three U.S. B-24s that had had to land on Turkish soil as they were returning to North Africa from bombing raids over Ploesti, Romania. U.S. officials in Cairo asked PAA-Africa to help. PAA's response was to take one of its civilian aircraft (which was looking much like a U.S. military aircraft in those days) and repaint it to resemble a commercial aircraft in which Willkie could travel to Turkey.

A suitable DC-3 was located from the PAA-Africa flight line and, over the weekend, all the army insignia were removed from the plane. A rectangular white panel was painted above the windows on each side of the aircraft and the

Wendell Willkie, speaking with the help of a hand-held microphone, urged PAA employees in Accra to join the U.S. Army and remain in Africa to support the war effort. By August 1942, control of the trans-Africa air route was shifting from PAA-Africa to the U.S. Army.

words "Pan American Airways System" painted in blue letters inside the panels. A large blue "U.S." was painted on white background under the left wing and a large blue "PAA" was painted on white background under the right wing. A fictitious "NC" number replaced the military identification number on the aircraft and PAA's logo was painted on both sides of the nose. As a final touch, the PAA staff secured several wicker chairs to the retaining rings in the floor of the aircraft so the passengers could travel in relative comfort.

On Monday, Willkie and his official party of two left Heliopolis for Ankara, Turkey, in their newly civilianized aircraft. PAA-Africa Captain Tom Collins was in command of the flight, which made its way up the eastern coast of the Mediterranean with stops at Lydda and Aleppo, before flying over the Taurus Mountains to reach Ankara. After their return to Cairo, Willkie continued his round-the-world journey in the *Gulliver*. The DC-3 was repainted and released back to normal service on the trans-Africa air route.

Other VIP Visitors

King George II of Greece passed through Cairo on board a PAA-Africa aircraft late in the spring of 1942. Several other VIPs transited through central Africa in the early days of the route. Eve Currie, Clare Booth Luce, and Madam Chiang Kai-shek were some of the more famous of the few women to pass through the route. Madame Chiang came through Africa on several occasions as she made several war-time visits to Washington, D.C., in her own C-54. She required extra security including specially prepared and tested meals.

Women in the camps posed special logistical problems for the PAA staff. Although there were some British nurses in Accra, work on the Africa air route was essentially a man's job and it was accomplished in a man's world.

King George II of Greece arriving on a PAA aircraft at Almaza Airport (Cairo) in June 1942. The purpose of his journey across Africa was to travel to Washington, D.C., to meet with President Roosevelt.

PAA-Africa Bequeaths an Air Route to the Allies

Perhaps the full impact of PAA-Africa, Ltd. on the war effort did not manifest itself until the airline closed its doors and ended its operation, flying its last missions late in 1942, as Anglo-American invasion forces were coming ashore in North Africa. On 8 November 1942, General Eisenhower led the amphibious landings in French Morocco and Algeria. The PAA-Africa installations already in place were key to the success of the follow-on transport and ferry missions accomplished by the U.S. Army Air Force and the air forces of the Allies.

The rush was on to deliver more tactical aircraft and additional supplies to the new combat front, with vital war cargoes arriving from the United States: bomb fuses, aircraft spare parts, foodstuffs, and medicines. Official U.S. Army war records show that from January 1943 through June 1944, 4,299 tactical and transport aircraft were ferried across Africa for delivery to U.S. and Allied military forces. Besides the aircraft ferry traffic, the Army's Air Transport Command in Accra handled thousands of additional airlift missions carrying mail, general cargo, and passengers to eastern Europe, the Middle East, and India. Thus, the level of flight operations grew to a rate never before observed on the African continent. Landings at Accra Air Base, for the period January 1943 through June 1945, totaled 10,148.

The activity represented by these figures was in stark contrast with the austere aviation infrastructure that was in place when PAA-Africa started its work in October 1941. The pioneering construction and the superb (even though often improvised) operational organization converted a tentative and risky resupply mission across Africa into almost a routine air service. By this achievement, Pan American Airways made a major contribution to the war effort, and in so doing, immeasurably influenced the course of the Second World War.

An aerial view of ATC's Headquarters at Accra Air Base in 1943.
PAA-Africa Ltd. had taken over the austere airport in October 1941 and
built a modern air terminal. (National Archives)

Military Take-Over

Predictably, with the United States no longer merely a sympathetic supporter of the Allied cause, but now an active belligerent, the U.S. Army moved to take over total control of the trans-Africa route as the U.S. prosecution of the war kicked into high gear early in 1942. Most observers agreed that PAA-Africa, Ltd., was doing an excellent job of developing the route and its infrastructure, but from the purely military perspective of the generals in Washington, it made sense for the U.S. Army to take over the control. With war officially declared, there was no longer a need for commercial pretense. The military value of the route was evidenced by the growing number of U.S. Army Air Corps aircraft and personnel passing through central Africa. Realizing for the first time the importance of airlift in the evolving global conflict, the U.S. Army began to establish its own Air Transport Command and provided the airlift forces with an operational budget. The ATC became fully operational late in June 1942 under the command of General Harold L. George. Brigadier General Shepler W. Fitzgerald was given command of the Air Transport Command's Twenty-Sixth Ferrying Wing, Africa Middle East Wing, which included the Africa section of the route.

Several events and policy discussions took place early in 1942, which helped the Army to influence the final decision from the War Department to terminate PAA-Africa, Ltd.'s contract. First, the question of the use of civilian air crews in the war zone was being reconsidered. The experience of the PAA-

Brigadier General
Shepler W. Fitzgerald.
(National Archives)

Africa civilian air crews in Burma during April and May of 1942 certainly highlighted the potential pitfalls of placing civilians in combatant positions. Second, British colonial officials in the region, as well as Air Ministry officials in London, were never really happy with having an American commercial air carrier operating in what they considered to be their sphere of influence. The British were concerned about their commercial prospects in Africa after the war and they did not like to see the Americans becoming firmly established in the region. Development of the mineral wealth of Africa was at stake, as well as the newly-located oil reserves in the Middle East. The British aviation press was particularly vocal in opposition to the use of an American commercial air carrier in Africa. And finally, some British officials were worried about the potential impact of a large American civilian presence in Africa, and its effect on African nationalism which was already in its nascent stages in the African colonies.

The Salalah Incident

These civilian-military rivalries were responsible for several flare-ups of outright animosity. One such problem developed in Salalah in June 1942. PAA-Africa ground crews arrived, unannounced to the Sultan, to establish a refueling station. To make matters worse, these individuals reportedly proceeded to break every local custom in the book, for example, looking at the Sultan's women, stealing the Sultan's water, and chasing the Sultan's foxes with a jeep. At the request of the British, as well as the Sultan, PAA's civilians were removed from the station by August and replaced by U.S. Army personnel. The episode was viewed quite differently from the PAA-Africa side. As the British had the contractual responsibility to obtain host country approvals for all PAA-Africa operations why had they failed to do so? There were also reports of attempts by the British commercial air carrier, B.O.A.C., which was still flying in the region with aircraft configured with civilian amenities, to pressure passengers to use it rather than to use the airlift provided by PAA-Africa. Allegations were also made that the latter was placing extra passengers and commercial cargo on some of its dedicated military support flights. Details aside, the prospect of post-war commercial rivalry between the Americans and the British no doubt played a significant role in the decision to militarize the route.

Additionally, Juan Trippe was falling out of favor in Washington. Many members of the Roosevelt Administration did not approve of Mr. Trippe and his arrogant methods, which he used to maneuver his airline into a controlling position over all transoceanic flight operations, and indeed, eventually for round-the-world service and global dominance. There was a certain irony in this, as Trippe was the one who had first raised the idea for a modern civilian airline-type air route to cross Africa during a critical meeting in London with Winston Churchill. Trippe had offered Pan Am's services and resources at a time when the British were under siege and in dire need of the kind of assistance that only Pan American, because of its resources and experience, could provide.

The U.S. Army Prepares

By early February 1942, the U.S. Army was already laying the groundwork to take over control of the Trans-Africa Air Route.

In a memorandum to Mr. Rownell, Special Assistant to the Assistant Secretary of War for Air, Brig. General Robert Olds laid out his belief that:

> ... the militarization of lines of air supply communication is an inevitable necessity in the prosecution of the war. These routes must be kept open at all costs. They constitute the only means whereby large combat aircraft can be transported to distant air theaters inasmuch as it is totally impossible to deck-load 4-engined bombers, for example. Sea routes for cargo boats have not been possible of establishment with the necessary guarantees of security to insure continuity of operations.

General Olds went on to explain that:

> Runway additions, reinforcements, additional communications, weather and housing facilities are needed now. These augmented

U.S. Army Air Corps mechanics, assigned to PAA-Africa in Karachi in July 1942, pose in front of a C-47. PAA maintenance representative Joe Patrick is in the middle.

facilities can be provided by the Army Corps of Engineers with funds now available in the Air Corps Ferrying Command budget.

The Air Transport Command listed the following reasons why the route should be militarized:

1. The need for unification of control and supervision.
2. Diplomatic and political considerations.
3. Securing of personnel.
4. Elimination of civilians in combat areas.
5. Working of civilians and soldiers side-by-side.
6. Necessity for military discipline over all personnel.
7. Relative availability of supplies.

In May 1942, Ferrying Command requested that PAA-Africa, Ltd. should provide detailed documentation and reports on all its operational activities. These monthly reports were to include manifests of cargoes and passengers, the amount of mail carried, a summary of the number of trips operated, and of the mileage and hours flown. PAA-Africa management agreed to this request and instructed all stations to comply. This reporting requirement followed an episode in mid-March when the War Department alleged that a PAA Clipper transported unauthorized commercial cargo and passengers in addition to military cargo en route to Lagos.

PAA-Africa Contract Extension

On 19 June 1942, the original PAA-Africa contract was extended to 15 August, with an option for the War Department to extend it to 15 December 1942. On 25 July, the Department notified PAA-Africa, Ltd. that the contract would be terminated on 15 December.

By September, it became more difficult for the company to provide all the required services with a work force that was being gradually stripped away

Major General Robert Olds, Air Corps, 1942. (National Archives)

by the military, as employees were transferring directly into military service. At the same time, all personnel replacement actions for the departing civilians had been put on hold because the contract was not going to be extended. Likewise, the military side was having difficulties in obtaining qualified manpower and there were some ambiguities as to whether or not the military or the civilian contractor was to perform certain tasks during the transition period. To complicate matters, the army wanted most of the employees to accept commissions or enlist in the U.S. Army. As an inducement to accept a military position, many men were given vacation time by the Army if they agreed. Thus, the working relationship between the military and its civilian contractor was becoming strained.

General Fitzgerald was given orders which designated him as the authorized representative of the Contracting Office and he exercised total control over the contractor's compliance activities. On 25 August 1942, he sent a letter to John Yeomans in Accra, advising him that PAA-Africa, Ltd. should suspend all service north and west of Takoradi, effective 30 August 1942. On 31 August, the Accra airfield was officially designated as the U.S. Army Air Base at Accra and Colonel Charles D. McAllister was assigned as the first Base Commander.

The 15 September edition of the *Africa News Letter*, PAA-Africa's internal—and to a large extent informal—publication issued to families and friends of employees, announced that the extension to the original contact would expire on 15 December 1942. The newsletter stated that

> ...the Army will transfer the operation of the route to the Army Air Force Transport Command and Brigadier General Fitzgerald, who is already in Africa with his staff, will assume control of the entire operation.

The report also stated that:

> ... many individuals may be asked to extend past 15 December in order to complete construction projects that are now under way, but will not be completed prior to mid-December.

Friction in Accra

In September, additional signs of friction began to show between PAA-Africa, Ltd. management and the U.S. Army's Air Transport Command leadership. Several events and personality clashes led to some rather harsh words from both sides. Delays were encountered as the Air Transport Command attempted to locate personnel for the scheduled 15 December changeover. General Fitzgerald felt that it was within his authority to order the PAA-Africa civilians to stay on the job in Africa after their individual contract expiration dates. As a result, the General refused to allow one PAA-Africa civilian, Santos Ceyanes, to leave Africa. When Assistant Manager James Smith, Jr., objected to this, General Fitzgerald requested that Smith be withdrawn at once. After several days of continued discussion, Smith and Fitzgerald managed to reach a better understanding of each party's respective manning problems. General Fitzgerald then withdrew his request for Smith's withdrawal from Accra. Ceyanes was authorized to leave Africa and a joint staff meeting was established, whereby the various problems facing the rapidly growing military and the rapidly dwindling civilian communities could be discussed. But not all the coordination problems were solved.

Smith spent much of his time in September counseling his men about the pros and cons of switching to the military system. There were ambiguities in ATC's contracts of employment, such as the length of the contract, pay and insurance, and workers' compensation. General Fitzgerald objected strenuously to a written statement that Smith made to his men about the possibilities of re-employment with Pan American in the United States. The General claimed that Smith was attempting to take personnel away from him; and things went downhill from there. Smith wrote to his home office that:

> Needless to say, there has been some friction between military personnel and civilians from time to time. Our personnel feel that they have been pushed around considerably, which is undoubtedly true. For example, the quarters made available to them by the Army since the camp was taken over are very much inferior to those which we provided. The men also do not feel that they can accomplish very much working to Army specifications and under Army procedures, because of their lack of familiarity with these.

On 21 October, General Fitzgerald and his Africa Middle East Wing, Air Transport Command, assumed responsibility for the Communications Department, the Maintenance Department (with the exception of those activities relating to Stores and Supplies), and the activities carried on under the jurisdiction of the Chief Pilot of PAA-Africa, Ltd. All other functions, such as flight operations, medical, transportation, construction, and commissary, remained the responsibility of PAA-Africa, Ltd.

Pan Am Staff Join the Army

The actual process of militarization continued incrementally through the fall of 1942. In a "PAA-Africa Militarization-Progress Report," dated 9 November 1942, management reported that on 24 July, George Kraigher (Operations Manager) was the first PAA employee to be commissioned as a Lt. Col. in the Army Air Corps. Additionally, 40 Reserve Officers serving with PAA-Africa had been called to active duty, 99 PAA-Africa non-reservists had been commissioned, and 13 employees had signed civilian contracts with the Army. Company records indicate that 34 percent of the employees entered the Army by 7 November. Between 2 September and 7 November, 250 employees elected to return to the United States.

More Friction

George Kraigher's commissioning did not go over well with the company, particularly when, five days after the event, Kraigher and John Yeomans, the company's Assistant Manager who was also commissioned, issued a lengthy memorandum entitled, "Reasons for Militarization of PAA-Africa, Ltd.", which represented their personal views on the issue. Vice President Frank Gledhill was quick to reply formally to the Army with a nine-page rebuttal, wherein he attempted to identify the fallacies in the Kraigher/Yeomans memorandum. The rebuttal was of little consequence and the militarization process continued.

By mid-November, PAA-Africa, Ltd. transmitted orders to all Airport Managers to begin removing, or painting out, all indications of PAA-Africa, Ltd. ownership on equipment and facilities. At those locations where the PAA-Africa Airport Manager had already been commissioned in the Army, the handling of this requirement was requested to occur, "at the convenience of the Airport Manager."

Also in November 1942, General Fitzgerald stirred up a hornet's nest of controversy when he complained, in a memorandum to Assistant Manager James Smith, that he had received reports that PAA-Africa personnel were, "laying down on the job along the line." Until this time, and in spite of the top-level differences, the relationship between PAA and the U.S. Army at the working level had been thought to be exemplary. But General Fitzgerald pulled no punches as he included in his letter a quotation from the Judge Advocate General's Office about the "... amenability (liability) of PAA personnel in Africa to military law."

PAA-Africa, Ltd. launched an immediate investigation and found that two employees had indeed been missing from their work stations at the

Hydraulic Shop in Accra. Both individuals were immediately relieved of their positions. The investigation also found that the core allegations were based mainly on hearsay, or based on isolated personality conflicts between individuals of PAA-Africa and U.S. Army personnel stationed along the route. In an internal PAA-Africa memorandum, Smith described the situation that he found to exist at one of the larger stations, Cairo:

> ... particular instance which he had in mind was one at Cairo involving maintenance work. At that station the Army has 25 maintenance men and Pan American 4. ...Captain Sicard (chief of Army maintenance) stated that the 4 Pan American personnel were doing their work well, and the fact that he cannot spare these men, although he has 25 Army mechanics, certainly indicates the value of the services which these Pan American men are rendering in Cairo...

Smith concluded that:

> ... the best procedure is for us to devote our attention to assisting the Army in every way possible. The value of such assistance as we may be able to render can best be judged by third parties traveling over the line.

Deadline

On 15 December, as the contract officially expired, Air Transport Command officials in Accra identified about 40 PAA-Africa civilian employees that the Army wished to retain in Africa for an undetermined period. Most of them were radio operators and other technicians for whom the Air Transport Command had not received replacements. The final scheduled flight by PAA-Africa, Ltd. was completed by Captain Dwight L. Shrum when he arrived in Accra on 12 December 1942 on a flight from Teheran. His co-pilot was a U.S. Army Air Corps pilot.

The confusion over operational control did not cease at the stroke of midnight on 15 December. Not until 22 December did General Fitzgerald write to the Commanding General, Air Transport Command, that "Pursuant to the terms of the original contract and its extension between the Government of the United States and Pan-American-Africa, Ltd., this contract terminated at midnight on 15 December, 1942."

The official army records show that 148 men from PAA-Africa, Ltd., were commissioned into the U.S. Army during this militarization process. These included:

Lieutenant Colonel	1
Majors	7
Captains	26
1st Lieutenants	72
2nd Lieutenants	<u>42</u>
Total	<u>148</u>

Additionally, 40 Reserve Officers employed by PAA-Africa were ordered to active duty in Africa. Colonel Kraigher, Colonel Yeomans, and Major Sherman stayed with the Air Transport Command and eventually became Acting Sector Commanders. Colonel Yeomans died in the line of duty.

Most of the PAA-Africa employees who declined to take the U.S. Army's offer of commissions or enlistments returned to the United States where they were offered positions with Pan American or other U.S. airlines.

Several employees (including the co-author of this book) were offered assignments with the new Pan American Airways-Africa Orient Division and returned to Africa. Some joined the U.S. Navy and one went to work as a welder with Johnson, Drake and Piper in Massawa, Eritrea, working on dry docks.

Militarization did not immediately relieve all the strains between the former PAA-Africa personnel and the newly-arriving army personnel. In the eyes of many of the army individuals who had to complete the difficult training at the Officer Candidate School (O.C.S.) or Officer Training School

Some of the civilian pilots donned military uniforms and remained in Africa to work for Uncle Sam. (L to R) Lt. Bob Carstensen, Lt. Bob Halley, Lt. Ross Herman and Lt. C.F. Linenbach shown here taking a break and visiting the pyramids in Cairo in 1943.

(O.T.S.), the PAA-Africa personnel were promoted to positions out of proportion to their actual military experience or qualifications. Examples of at least one stock clerk and one manual laborer commissioned as majors did not sit well with the newly-arriving soldiers. Likewise, some of the PAA-Africa personnel thought that they had been hoodwinked into accepting lower-paying positions and that all the new folks arriving were so inexperienced that they too had been given ranks well beyond their military value. A U.S. Army report, originally classified as "Secret," goes a little further in describing the problem:

> Pan American Airways Africa Ltd., built the Base and its person-
> nel in a measure cast the mold in which the Base was to operate
> even after the assumption of the functions by the Air Transport
> Command. This condition built up rivalries, engendered some-
> thing close to hatred among civilians and the military, and creat-
> ed a morale problem which took many months to solve.

Dissolution

The PAA-Africa, Ltd., corporate structure did not cease to exist when flight operations in Africa came to a halt on 15 December 1942. The corporation continued to exist, at least on paper, until 20 October 1952, when a Certificate of Dissolution was filed in the State of Delaware.

Furthermore, the presence of Pan American Airways in Africa did not end with the termination of PAA-Africa, Ltd.'s contract. A new division, PAA-Africa-Orient Division, was created, and it received a contract from the newly-formed Air Transport Command to provide transport delivery services across Africa and eventually to the Far East. The Africa-Orient Division would continue to fly transport aircraft across Africa and gain widespread recognition for its "Cannonball Express" service to the Far East. But the old PAA-Africa, Ltd. was now history and the U.S. Army was, for the first time, solely in control of all the American flight operations on the trans-Africa air route.

Their Legacy—
Alive Today

"Victory in Egypt came by the Takoradi route."
—Philip Guedalla (British Historian)

V
ictory in Egypt may well have been won by the Takoradi route. But the above statement begs another question: what role did the entire trans-Africa air route, from the South Atlantic, across Africa, through Egypt and the Middle East, to India and China, have on the outcome of the total war effort of the Allies? The work accomplished by PAA-Africa played a critical role, not only for victory in Egypt, but for the entire allied war effort. The results of battles fought in southern Europe, eastern Europe, and Asia were all affected by the presence of and contributions made by the trans-Africa air route. PAA-Africa established one of America's first "bare-base" flight operations in terrain that was considered by many to be impossible to allow routine flights. The company also set some important precedents in American aviation by transporting military supplies and personnel to combat zones around the world and conducting the first American air evacuation, using civilian air crews, to rescue Allied and U.S. military forces and to transfer civilian personnel out of harm's way.

The legacy of this relatively small group of U.S. civilians is hard to quantify, but not difficult to verify. A document found at the U.S. Army's Historical Institute at Carlisle Barracks, Pennsylvania, shows that between August 1942 and March 1944, 11,386 military aircraft passed through the South Atlantic portion of the trans-Africa air route, carrying 101,961 military personnel. This does not include the aircraft the British moved through Takoradi. The total number of movements will probably never be known, but the trans-Africa air route was recognized as the most heavily scheduled "air track" in the world. Although PAA-Africa, Ltd. had departed from the African scene by the end of December 1942, its pioneering work had established a viable, modern transport service across central Africa that set the stage for expanded activity and enabled the U.S. military to operate globally with such efficiency during the remaining days of the Second World War.

The legacy of PAA-Africa, Ltd. and its wartime work transcends the period of the Allies' ultimate victory achieved in 1945. PAA-Africa's actions and accomplishments set precedents for the future use of the nation's civilian aviation assets in support of U.S. military airlift requirements. The memory of PAA-Africa is still alive today as we look at the special relationship currently existing between America's civilian airlines and the U.S. military.

Forging a Civilian/Military Aviation Partnership

Early in the 1940s, the U.S. military transportation planners realized that the nation's civilian aviation companies had the ability to support air missions that the U.S. military was not capable of doing on its own. Before 1941, the U.S. Army had never successfully deployed aviation units to provide logistical support to ground troops or aviation units operating away from their home bases. Indeed, there had been little need to do so. But in 1941 we witnessed, for the first time, a U.S. civilian aviation company stepping in to provide airlift and logistics support to American and Allied combat forces. Thus, PAA-Africa demonstrated the effectiveness of a civilian-military aviation partnership, one that continues to this day. Such cooperation was quite evident during the Korean and Vietnam wars, when many U.S. airlines, scheduled (including Pan American) and non-scheduled, provided substantial airlift support for the combatant U.S. armed forces. Modern-day military planners continue to rely heavily on elements of the American civil aviation sector to provide airlift support.

The Civilian Reserve Air Fleet (CRAF) is the formal institution, created by the U.S. Government in 1951, to perpetuate this partnership. American commercial airlines continue the proud tradition, first exercised by Pan American Airways early in the 1940s, of providing civilian airlift support, under contract to the Air Mobility Command of the United States Air Force. The most recent, highly visible military operation depending on the participation of American civil airlines, or CRAF program, was Operation Desert Shield (and Storm) during the Gulf War. The success achieved by the U.S. military and the members of the U.S.-sponsored Coalition in the Gulf can be attributed largely to the efforts of the civilian airlines and their air crews who airlifted the fighting men and women and their supplies to the Persian Gulf. During a May 1991 speech to the Aero Club of Washington, paying tribute to the "Aviators of Desert Storm," the Honorable Diane K. Morales, then Deputy Assistant Secretary of Defense (Logistics), stated:

*THEN: U.S.
military personnel
prepare to embark
on a PAA-Africa
flight across
Africa in 1941.
This was a
military contract
operation.*

*NOW: U.S. military personnel prepare to embark on a Civilian Reserve Air Fleet
(CRAF) mission from the Persian Gulf in 1991. (Courtesy: Northwest Airlines)*

Since the operation began last August, the Military Airlift Command (MAC) and their civil air carrier partners have flown almost 23,000 missions—3,000 with passengers and 20,000 with cargo. Fully 22 percent of these have been flown by the crews of the civil reserve air fleet—all of whom deserve to be standing beside the military "Aviators of Desert Storm" we are honoring today. I would like to focus on this fleet (CRAF) today partly because they have not received the recognition that our more visible military aviators have and because these aircraft are such a crucial part of our DOD airlift force and deterrence posture. Secretary Cheney has made it clear that we will continue to rely to the extent possible on the civil sector as a permanent member of our defense team.

Morales went on to add:

Two-thirds of all the passengers and one-fifth of all the air cargo were moved to the Gulf by civil aircraft. More significantly, thus far, during the redeployment, 87% of the passengers and 43% of the cargo has been transported by civil air carriers. We clearly could not have accomplished our mission without CRAF—and the same will be true in future major regional contingencies.

Morales's comments concerning the nation's failure to recognize the contributions of the civilian airlifters in Desert Storm is particularly poignant. As in the case of Desert Storm, the PAA employees who served heroically during the Second World War received little recognition for their efforts. The pioneering PAA-Africa in 1941, the supplemental carriers during the Korean War of 1954, the airlines of the Vietnam War of the late 1960s, or the civilian crews participating in Operation Desert Storm in 1991: the non-military element of all these is often overlooked when the nation distributes praise and the historians chronicle the events in our aviation history books.

Evacuation Missions

In another landmark event of the Second World War, the U.S. Government used civilian air crews for the first time to conduct the evacuation by air of combatants and non-combatant civilians. PAA-Africa's scheduled evacuation flights from Burma, in May 1942, set a precedent for American civilian air crews to participate in government-sanctioned air evacuations from combat

Evacuation operations at the gate to Cairo's Heliopolis airport on 1 July 1942. The adding machine on the trunk of the army vehicle and the scale were used to determine passenger and baggage weight for computing the aircraft weight-and-balance. The U.S. Army tank crew, wearing side-arms and standing under the porch, had been operating with British tank units in the desert and had been ordered back to the United States to serve as instructors in tank tactics.

zones or out of harm's way. As detailed earlier in this text, PAA-Africa crews were called upon to participate in the evacuation of civilian refugees and wounded Allied soldiers from Burma. Several months later, in July 1942, PAA-Africa's civilian air crews were again charged by the U.S. Government to conduct evacuation operations. This time PAA-Africa evacuated civilians and military personnel from Cairo, Egypt.

Since 1942, civilian air crews have been called upon to make dozens of similar rescue flights to evacuate thousands of American citizens and foreign nationals from virtually every corner of the globe. The most recent example occurred in May 1998. The U.S. Government again turned to civilian air lines to conduct an "ordered departure" of non-combatants from Indonesia and Eritrea, two countries where security conditions deteriorated rapidly. The U.S. State Department and the Department of Defense teamed together to charter commercial airliners to evacuate American civilians to safe havens in neighboring countries in southeast Asia and Africa.

The Air Route and the Africans

PAA-Africa's legacy should also be measured by its lasting influence on the lives of the African people. At one time, PAA-Africa employed more than 1,500 Africans to work at the main operating base in Accra. Many more were employed at the other stations along the route. For most of them, this was their first contact with non-European white people. Studies record that many Africans were affected by participation in the Second World War, mainly soldiers who had left their homes to join the British and French armed forces, and went to far-off lands to fight. But little has been written about the considerable influence on those who remained in their homelands, and were exposed to a wartime western culture, a culture of which the Pan American personnel represented a substantial element.

The lasting effect of the opening of the modern east-west air route across Africa on the growth of nationalism among the embryonic independence movements spreading across Africa in the 1940s–1950s is a matter of speculation. The improved aviation infrastructure no doubt played an important role in the spread of nationalistic fervor across Africa. Did African leaders such as Kwama Nkrumah in Ghana and Félix Houphouët-Boigny in the Ivory Coast benefit from these aviation facilities provided by Americans, as they moved their countries towards independence?

These airfields, developed by PAA-Africa and used along the route from Bathurst to Accra to El Fasher to Khartoum and Cairo, are still very active today in 1999. For example, Bathurst has been an alternate emergency landing site for the American Space Shuttle; Accra is the home field for Ghana Airways and the Ghana Air Force; El Fasher is still a vital refueling site for smaller aircraft flying across Africa; and Cairo's Almaza Airfield is still serving as an Egyptian Air Force Base. Only one or two of the airfields have been moved or closed since 1942. These airfields, which played host to P-40s, B-24s and B-17s fifty-seven years ago, are still serving as vital air links on a continent where aviation is sometimes the only means of transportation available.

A Grateful Nation Recognizes Her Heroes—Finally

During its term of duty in Africa, from several months before the U.S. entered the Second World War as a belligerent nation, Pan American's role was somewhat ambiguous. It performed tasks that were para-military in their objectives, and equally so in their operations.

Not until July 1992 did the men of PAA-Africa receive official U.S. Government recognition for their patriotism, sacrifices, and their contributions to the American war effort. After several years of intense advocacy work, led by retired Pan American flight engineer Ernie Colant and his wife Scharleen, the Department of Defense Civilian/Military Service Review Board recommended to the Secretary of the Air Force that the men of PAA-Africa, Ltd. be considered to have served on "active duty" and given official recognition, as a group, for their wartime service.

56th Anniversary gathering of the PAA-Africa Ltd. alumni group in Treasure Island, Florida, 15-18 April 1997.

(Left to Right)
Front Row-Andy Dawson, Tom Hoopes, Miller Logan, Ed Young, Tom Flanagan, George Clayton, Ray Tirado

Second Row-Bernard Sherwood, Armond Droz, Gordon Hill, Hank LaVelle, Joe Hughes, George Banton, Roy Hackett, Richard Miller, Bob Roberts, Bob Nelson, Bob Mueller

Third Row-Bob Murphy, Dean Newell, Harry Jenkins, Tom Carroll, Harry Bernard, Bart Hewitt, Peter Goutiere, Ed Frankiewicz, Arnold Graff, Wes Spencer, Art Swanson

Attendees missing from photo: Jack Hudson, Sam Marchinsky, Ed Shaffer

The Board reported that,

... the group defined as "U.S. Civilian Flight Crew and Aviation Ground Support Employees of Pan American World Airways and Its Subsidiaries and Affiliates, Who Served Overseas as a Result of Pan American's Contract with the Air Transport Command and Naval Air Transport Service During the period December 14, 1941 through August 14, 1945," should be considered active duty for the purposes of all laws administered by the Veterans Administration.

Determinations of active military service such as these are made on the extent to which civilian groups were under the control of U.S. Armed Forces in support of a military operation or mission during an armed conflict. The Board determined that this group satisfied practically all of the criteria which indicate that U.S. Armed Forces exerted control over the group as if their members were military personnel.

The Assistant Secretary of Air Force, The Honorable J. G. Cooper, under the provisions of DODD (Department of Defense Directive) 1000.20, "Active Duty Service Determinations for Civilian or Contractual Groups" and Public Law 95-202, signed the designation letter on 16 July 1992. Thus, all civilian employees of PAA-Africa, Ltd., who served overseas and met specified criteria, are entitled to receive an Honorable Discharge from the U.S. Air Force and establish their status as military veterans of the United States of America.

The PAA-Africa Ltd. alumni group has been instrumental in spreading the word about the "Veteran Status" designation among its membership. To receive the Honorable Discharge and Veteran Status designation, each individual employee must submit an official application form (DD Form 2168) to the U.S. Air Force. By early 1995, more than 70 members of the alumni group had applied for and were awarded the Honorable Discharge by the U.S. Air Force.

Receiving the Honorable Discharge certificate and achieving "Veteran Status" has proved, to differing degrees, a form of "closure" for many of the civilians who served their nation with PAA-Africa, Ltd. Several months before Pearl Harbor many of them left the shores of the United States to go to war. They received scant recognition for their wartime efforts. At last, they are receiving official thanks from their government for their valuable wartime service. Now, as these men describe to their grandchildren and great-grandchildren the work they did in far-away Africa during the Second World War, they can back up their words with something more tangible. They have it in writing from a grateful nation.

Appendix A
PAA Recruiting Letter

PAN AMERICAN AIRWAYS SYSTEM

GENERAL OFFICES, CHRYSLER BUILDING, 135 EAST 42ND STREET, NEW YORK, N. Y.

Dear Sir♦

We now have positions open for pilots in Africa, the Middle East and other overseas points with our transport operation of multi-engine equipment.

Those applicants acceptable as student pilots receive $100.00 per month, plus $6.00 a day expenses while in the United States. On assignment to foreign duty, pilot receives $200.00 per month plus all maintenance.

Applicants acceptable as co-pilots receive $250.00 per month plus $6.00 a day expenses in the United States. On assignment to foreign duty they receive 350.00 per month plus all maintenance.

Pilots acceptable as captains receive $604.00 per month, plus $6.00 a day expenses in the United States. On assignment to foreign duty they receive $755.00 per month plus all maintenance.

If you are interested, are unemployed and have a release without prejudice from your former employer, this is your authorization to proceed to New York for an interview and medical examination. Report to Room 4408 of the Chrysler Building.

We will reimburse your traveling expenses by train, bus or automobile. Please retain all receipts for traveling expenses.

Please wire us, stating exactly when you will arrive in New York.

Very truly yours,

PAN AMERICAN AIRWAYS SYSTEM

Joseph J. Ince

Appendix B

Fleet List for PAA-Africa

PLANE	FROM	DATE	AIRCRAFT HOURS	ENGINE SERIAL	ENGINE HOURS	TO	DATE	AIRCRAFT HOURS	ENGINE SERIAL	ENGINE HOURS
N16082	E.A.L.	2-27-42	192:09	79031/79032	192:09	RAF CAIRO	4-10-42		79031/79032	
N16094	E.A.L.	1-20-42	1333:09	79027/79028	50:25	RAF CAIRO	4-10-42		79027/79023	212:54/600:19
N16117	P.A.A.	11-17-41	6132:17	25445/25446	94:51/96:31	DESTROYED	4-19-42	6646:05	79025/25446	
N17313	T.W.A.	1-20-42	1350:39	79029/79030	39:25	RAF CAIRO	4-20-42	13079:02	79029/79030	379:30
N21750	C.C.A.	11-10-41	3953:13	20374/29109	46:00/71:00	DESTROYED	3-16-42	4370:21	20374/29109	465:00/490:00
N25623	N.W.A.	10-4-41	1550:00	1529/3103	100:00	DESTROYED	4-15-42	2396:51	11601/11600	758:30
N33642	U.A.L.	10-3-41	100:00	8773	100:00	RAF FRE	9-2-42	906:55	11903	58:40
N33653	A.A.L.	11-2-42	402:02	34569/34570	402:02	RAF CAIRO	5-6-42	867:34	12299	22:24
N33655	A.A.L.	10-20-41	443:23	29709/29674	67:02/52:32	RAF CAIRO	2-1-42		79035/79023	
N33675	P.C.A.	11-17-41	639:56	34516/34620	67:03/26:30	RAF CAIRO	4-17-42	566:33	34516/34620	566:33
42-6505	CITY SER.	2-26-42	230:45	5971/5972	230:45	ATC ACCRA	10-16-42	543:00	12300/14904	526:00/543:00
42-14297	A.T.C.	3-3-42	76:52	11916/11918	76:52	RAF CAIRO	4-7-42	207:37	11916/11916	207:37
42-14298	A.T.C.	3-24-42	72:16	11919/11920	72:16	ATC KRA	4-2-42	130:26	11919/11920	130:26
41-20057	A.T.C. NEW	3-4-42	86:14	15465/15467	86:14	ATC ACCRA	10-16-42	1190:42	15269/14966	455:11
41-20058	A.T.C.	2-20-42	167:00	10063/10064	167:00	ATC ACCRA	10-16-42	254:33	NO ENGINES	-
41-20059	A.T.C.	2-21-42	173:20	10070/10072	173:20	ATC ACCRA	10-16-42	1466:19	13212/14092	663:50
41-20078	A.T.C. NEW	2-3-42	66:12	11715/11722	66:12	ATC ACCRA	10-16-42	1029:46	3103/1529	201:03
41-20079	A.T.C. NEW	2-3-42	62:23	11719/11723	62:23	ATC ACCRA	10-16-42	447:53	11719/11723	447:53

PLANE	FROM	DATE	AIRCRAFT HOURS	ENGINE SERIAL	ENGINE HOURS	TO	DATE	AIRCRAFT HOURS	ENGINE SERIAL	ENGINE HOURS
41-20080	A.T.C. NEW	2-3-42	64:30	12839 / 12843	64:30	ATC ACCRA	10-16-42	1303:01	14036 / 13311	589:42
41-20081	A.T.C. NEW	2-20-42	92:47	11726 / 11727	92:47	RAF KRA	4-25-42	384:08	11726 / 11727	384:08
41-20084	A.T.C. NEW	2-23-42	62:12	12844 / 12849	62:12	ATC ACCRA	10-16-42	1247:18	13285 / 13279	403:51
41-20085	A.T.C. NEW	2-25-42	75:57	12824 / 12834	75:57	ATC ACCRA	10-16-42	747:34	14985 / 14987	1:30
41-20099	A.T.C. NEW	3-3-42	87:23	12937 / 12963	87:23	ITC ACCRA	10-16-42	1213:11	14078 / 13304	366:03
41-20101	A.T.C. NEW	3-9-42	82:23	12904	82:23	CNAC	4-12-42	197:09	12979 / 12904	197:09
41-20102	A.T.C. KRA	5-27-42	140:00	11714 / 11713	140:00	ATC ACCRA	10-16-42	765:54	14042 / 14807	765:54
41-20103	A.T.C. NEW	3-20-42	76:30	12997 / 13002	76:30	ATC ACCRA	10-16-42	723:36	13303 / 16591	261:23 / 723:36
41-20105	A.T.C. NEW	4-24-42	93:15	13006 / 13009	93:15	ATC ACCRA	10-16-42	820:22	15214 / 15211	109:40 / 820:22
41-20109	A.T.C. NEW	3-20-42	94:45	13034 / 13203	94:45	CNAC	5-12-42	138:20	13034 / 14075	138:20 / 35:11
41-20110	A.T.C. NEW	5-17-42	141:50	13219 / 13242	141:50	ATC ACCRA	10-16-42	801:13	15206 / 13252	001:13 / 173:51
41-20111	A.T.C. NEW	3-20-42	90:23	13253 / 13254	90:23	CNAC	6-5-42	420:00	13253 / 13254	420:00
41-20115	A.T.C. NEW	3-24-42	89:30	13263 / 13264	89:30	CNAC	6-5-42	420:00	13263 / 13264	420:00
41-20115	A.T.C. NEW	3-24-42	83:15	13273 / 13290	83:15	ATC ACCRA	10-16-42	1047:20	14985 / 14064	250:14
41-20117	A.T.C. NEW	3-24-42	89:09	13296 / 13297	89:09	ATC ACCRA	10-16-42	639:04	NO ENGINES	—

PLANE	FROM	DATE	AIRCRAFT HOURS	ENGINE SERIAL	ENGINE HOURS	TO	DATE	AIRCRAFT HOURS	ENGINE SERIAL	ENGINE HOURS
42-6455	A.T.C. NEW	5-21-42	97:40	13667	97:40	DESTROYED	7-12-42	369:41	13667	369:41
42-6457	A.T.C. NEW	6-4-42	68:30	13671	68:30	RAF CAIRO	8-1-42	390:00	13671	390:00
42-6458	A.T.C.	8-23-42	257:45	13678	257:45	ATC ABSEA	10-16-42	536:23	13678 13679	536:23
42-6462	A.T.C.	8-20-42	293:50	13679 13680 13632	293:50	ATC ACCRA	10-16-42	666:44	13680 13682 13242 14049	85:32 666:44
42-6467	A.T.C. NEW	6-4-42	85:55	13047 14049	85:55	ATC ACCRA	10-16-42	767:36	14101 14115	767:36
42-6470	A.T.C. NEW	6-8-42	96:37	14001 14115	96:37	ATC ERA	8-8-42	475:00	14025 14028	475:00
42-6471	A.T.C. NEW	6-6-42	75:35	14025 14028	75:35	ATC ERA	8-3-42	425:00	14031	425:00
42-6472	A.T.C. NEW	5-22-42	70:00	14031 14041 14043 14033	70:00	ATC ERA	9-3-42	600:00	14041 14048 14033	600:00
42-6492	A.T.C. NEW	6-24-42	95:25	12930 12954	95:25	ATC ACCRA	10-16-42	732:16	12930 12954 14140	732:16
41-7722	A.T.C. NEW	3-9-42	94:26	10039 9996	94:26	ATC ACCRA	10-16-42	825:11	14140 11907	36:30
41-7723	A.T.C. NEW	3-17-42	107:06	10025 15425	107:06	ATC ACCRA	10-16-42	1181:48	15876 14104	264:34
41-7725	A.T.C. NEW	3-9-42	89:14	10034 10030	89:14	ATC ACCRA	10-16-42	1063:36	13229 13247	263:53
41-7726	A.T.C. NEW	3-9-42	84:34	10045 10049	84:34	ATC ACCRA	10-16-42	1001:05	13290 16539	148:03
41-7727	A.T.C. NEW	3-21-42	88:28	9695 10040	88:28	ATC ERA	4-15-42	175:30	9695	175:30
41-7728	A.T.C. NEW	3-16-42	86:31	10024 10026	86:31	DESTROYED	5-25-42	400:00	10040 10024	400:00
41-7729	A.T.C. NEW	3-20-42	86:15	10065 10067	86:15	ATC ACCRA	10-16-42	938:44	10026 12301 13261	86:23 155:43
41-7730	A.T.C. NEW	3-9-42	84:32	10031 10037	84:32	ATC ACCRA	10-16-42	1064:57	16590 14029	217:13
41-7738	A.T.C. NEW	4-8-42	92:10	10477 10479	92:10	ATC ACCRA	10-16-42	527:15	10477 10479	527:15

PLANE	FROM	DATE	AIRCRAFT HOURS	ENGINE SERIAL	ENGINE HOURS	TO	DATE	AIRCRAFT HOURS	ENGINE SERIAL	ENGINE HOURS
41-7739	A.T.C. NEW	8-25-42	45:16	12446 12450	45:16	ATC ACCRA	10-16-42	346:52	12446 12450	346:52
41-7754	A.T.C. NEW	8-26-42	167:42	17401 17402	167:42	ATC ACCRA	10-16-42	448:25	17401 17482	448:25
41-7756	A.T.C. NEW	6-1-42	75:55	10518	75:55	ATC KRA	8-5-42	470:00	10517	470:00
41-7758	A.T.C. NEW	5-30-42	76:43	10510	76:43	ATC KRA	8-14-42	350:00	10510	350:00
41-7759	A.T.C. NEW	6-0-42	75:00	10464 10473	75:00	ATC KRA	8-11-42	450:00	10464 10473	450:00
41-7760	A.T.C. NEW	5-11-42	92:20	10482 10499	92:20	ATC ACCRA	10-16-42	804:01	10482 10499	804:01
41-7796	A.T.C. NEW	5-27-42	83:35	10513 10520	83:35	ATC KRA	8-7-42	500:00	10513 10520	500:00
41-7798	A.T.C. NEW	6-0-42	84:00	10955 10956	84:00	ATC ACCRA	10-16-42	743:47	10955 10956	743:47
41-7831	PAN-E 8-20-42		710:00	10516 10092	44:46	ATC ACCRA	10-16-42	363:10	10516 10092	363:10
41-7864	A.T.C. NEW	5-30-42	100:00	12460 12464	100:00	US ARMY OURA	9-1-42	500:00	12460 12464	500:00
41-7865	A.T.C. NEW	5-26-42	69:07	12830 12850	69:07	ATC KRA	9-9-42	590:00	12830 12850	590:00
41-38566	A.T.C. NEW	7-29-42	74:50	12847 12854	74:5	ATC ACCRA	10-16-42	519:33	12847 12854	519:33
41-38567	A.T.C. NEW	7-27-42	69:30	14223 14225	69:30	ATC ACCRA	10-16-42	503:53	14223 14225	503:53
41-38568	A.T.C. NEW	7-31-42	66:56	12940 12943	66:56	ATC ACCRA	10-16-42	555:03	12940 12943	555:03
41-38570	A.T.C. NEW	8-0-42	69:25	12947 12948	69:25	ATC ACCRA	10-16-42	416:16	12947 12948	416:16
41-38572	A.T.C. NEW	8-3-42	66:56	14218 14219	66:56	ATC ACCRA	10-16-42	468:12	14210 14219	468:12
41-38577	A.T.C. NEW	7-31-42	75:00	14224 14226	75:00	US ARMY OURA	9-25-42	400:00	14224 14226	400:00
41-38579	A.T.C. NEW	8-21-42	75:00	14090 14109 14863 14882	75:00	ATC ACCRA	10-16-42	306:29	14090 14109 14863 14882	306:29

PLANE	FROM	DATE	AIRCRAFT HOURS	ENGINE SERIAL	ENGINE HOURS	TO	DATE	AIRCRAFT HOURS	ENGINE SERIAL	ENGINE HOURS
41-30581	A.T.C. NEW	8-4-42	67:26	14849	67:26	ATC ACCRA	10-16-42	480:40	14849 14851	480:40
41-38502	A.T.C. NEW	8-5-42	80:00	14851	80:00	ATC ACCRA	8-6-42	80:00	14854 14855	80:00
41-38583	A.T.C. NEW	8-3-42	66:56	14854 14855	66:56	US ARMY CHERA	9-8-42	300:00	14833 14837	300:00
41-18400	A.T.C. NEW	8-16-42	66:56	14833 14837	66:56	ATC ACCRA	10-16-42	395:21	14239	395:21
41-18401	A.T.C. NEW	8-3-42	66:56	14239	66:56	ATC ACCRA	10-16-42	494:46	14242 14245 14246	494:46
41-18402	A.T.C. NEW	8-4-42	66:56	14242 14245 14246	66:56	ATC ACCRA	10-16-42	475:30	14739 14740	475:30
41-18403	A.T.C. NEW	8-21-42	75:00	14739 14740 14741 14749	75:00	ATC ACCRA	10-16-42	381:09	14741 14749	381:09
42-47373	A.T.C. NEW	7-22-42	66:56	13613 13621	66:56	ATC ACCRA	10-16-42	585:05	13613 13621	585:05
42-47376	A.T.C. NEW	7-22-42	66:56	14023 14024	66:56	ATC ACCRA	10-16-42	547:55	14023 14024	547:55
42-47377	A.T.C. NEW	7-21-42	66:56	14093 14109	66:56	ATC ACCRA	10-16-42	604:29	14093 14109	604:29
N3021 James Donahue, 9-7-41 New York			123:55	6203 6202	0	ATC ACCRA	10-16-42	370:35	6205 6206	0
NL6915 Boris Sergievski, 10-20-37 New York			No record	7005 7006	0	ATC ACCRA	10-17-42	669:30	12295 7086	10:40 139:30

Appendix C

Letter to Arab Peoples for Use by Downed Pilots

الى كل عربي كريم

السلام عليكم ورحمة الله وبركاته . وبعد نحامل هذا الكتاب ضابط
بجيش الولايات المتحدة الاميركية ، وهو ناصر الحكومة الأنكليزية
وصديق وفي لكافة الشعوب العربية . فنرجو أن تعاملوته بالعطف والاكرام .
وأن تحافظوا على حياته من كل طارئ ونأمل عند الاضطرار أن تقدموا له ما
يحتاج اليه من طعام وشراب ، وأن ترشدونه الى اقرب معسكر بريطاني .
وسنكافئكم مالياً بسخاء على ما تسدونه اليه من خدمات .
والسلام عليكم ورحمة الله وبركاته .
بأجازة من القيادة البريطانية العامة في الشرق .

To every noble Arab

Greetings and peace of Allah be upon you. The bearer of this letter is
an officer of the United States of America, assisting the British Govern-
nment and a faithful friend to all Arab Nations. We beg of you to treat
him well, guard his life from every harm and supply his needs of food
and drinks, and guide him to the nearest British encampment. You will
be rewarded generously in money for all your services. Peace and mercy
of Allah be upon you.

By a permit of the British High Command of the East.

USEFUL WORDS

English	Arabic	English	Arabic
American	Amrika-ni	Water	Moyah
American Flying Officer	Za-bit Amrika-ni Tye-yar	Food	A'-kl
Friend	Sa-hib, Sa-deek	Sick	Ma-reed

Take me to the English and you will be rewarded.
Khud-nee eind el-Ingleez, Ta-khud mu-ka-fa-a.

PAA Certificate of Identity

CERTIFICATE OF IDENTITY.   No. 65

    The bearer of this certificate, Mr. **L. R. Eagles** , is a non-combatant employee of Pan-America Africa, Ltd., which performs services for the military authorities of the United States of America. Being a civilian, he is entitled to the benefits provided for by Article 81 of the Geneva Convention concerning Prisoners of War.

        FOR THE COMMANDING GENERAL:

                            ROBERT W. STRONG
                            Colonel GSC.
                            Chief of Staff
                            U.S.Army Forces in
                            Central Africa.

Right
Thumbprint
of
Bearer.

TRANSLATION

TITRE D'IDENTITE

    Le porteur du présent titre, M....**L. R. Eagles**...........est un non-combattant, employé de la PAN-AMERICA-AFRICA LTD dont les services sont requis par les autorités militaires des Etats- Unis d'Amérique. En tant que civil, il est admis au bénéfice des dispositions de l' art. 81 de la Convention de Genève réglant le traitement des prisonniers de guerre.

TRANSLATION

AUSWEIS

    Inhaber diese Ausweises, Herr..**L. R. Eagles**..... gehört nicht zur Truppe. Er ist ein Angestellter der PAN-AMERICA - AFRICA G.M.B.H. deren Dienstleistungen von der Heeresverwaltung der Vereinigten Staten von Nordamerika angefordert sind. Als Zivilist hat er Anspruch auf alle Rechte die ihm im Sinne des Paragr. 81 des Genfer Abkommens über die Behandlung von Kriegs gefangenen zugesichert sind.

Appendix D

First Flight U.S. Air Mail Cover San Juan P.R.

First PANAIRMAIL Service: Egypt to U.S.A. First Day Cover

First PANAIRMAIL Service: Egypt to U.S.A. First Day Cover

Exhibit 1   165

Exhibit 1

Operations Order Number 397, 30 November 1942

AFRICA MIDDLE EAST WING, AIR TRANSPORT COMMAND
HEADQUARTERS TWELFTH FERRYING GROUP.
Office of the Commanding Officer

c/o Postmaster, Miami, Fla.

OPERATIONS ORDER)

. November 30,......19 42

NUMBER 397)

Par 6, Pursuant to authority contained in Ltr from the CG Hq AMEW,
dated October 12, 1942, subject: "Authority to Issue Travel Orders"
the following named Officers and EM will proceed in the following
listed aircraft :—

SERIAL No.	TYPE	FROM	TO
8399	C-47	Accra, Gold Coast	Karachi, India

From _____ TO _____
and return, making such intermediate stops as are necessary for the
performance of this mission.

Capt White   (PAA)

1st Lt. Arthur C. Anderson O-483526

In lieu of subs a flat per diem of ($6.00) six dollars per
day is auth while travelling by mil aircraft.

The duty to be performed being exceptional and requiring
more than seventy-two (72) hours to perform, a delay of not to
exceed thirty (30) days in any one place is hereby authorized.

TDN   AC 2397 P 96 - 02 A 0705 - 23.

Attached hereto and made a part hereof, is passenger manifest
showing names & destinations of all passengers, such list not being
authority for claim of per diem as authorized above.

By order of Lieutenant Colonel KRAIGHER :

MILTON H. CHAMPION
Major, Air Corps.,

(Operations Officer)

*This was a travel order for an officer taking a C-47 flight down from Accra to
Karachi. Per diem was $6.00 per day, and the duty was described as "exceptional"
and therefore permitting a delay "in any one place" of up to 30 days.*

Exhibit 2

PAA-Africa, Ltd. Pilot's Monthly Flight Time Statement

PAN AMERICAN AIRWAYS-AFRICA, LIMITED
PILOTS MONTHLY FLIGHT TIME STATEMENT.

Month_____September_____, 194_2_____   For _____FRANKIEWICZ, E. J.,_____

DAY	PLANE	ROUTE	NATURE OF FLIGHT Pro-ductive	Non-Pro-ductive	Total	Pilot	Co-Pilot	Night	Inst.
19	17729	ACR ACR	25		25		25		
8	17831	KRT ACR	820		820		820	140	
20	"	ACR URI	450		450		450		30
21	"	URI KRT	570		570		570	15	
22	"	KRT ADN	360		360		360		
23	"	ADN KRA	675		675		675		140
25	"	KRA HAB	675		675		675		
26	"	HAB RAY LYD	260		260		260		
27	"	LYD HEL	135		135		135		
19	18400	ACR TKD	60		60		60		
1c	"	TKA ACR	60		60		60		
29	20057	CAI KRT	350		350		350		
14	20099	ACR FSH	270		270		270	25	
14	"	FSH ACR	335		335		335		35
5	13867	CAI LUX	125		125		125		
6	"	LUX GUR	315		315		315		
7	"	GUR KRT	150		150		150		
1	34c00	ACR TKD ACR	120		120		120		
2	47374	ACR URI	455		455		455		30
3	"	URI KRT	535		535		535		
4	"	KRT CAI	380		380		380	180	

Total This Month			118:45		118:45		118:45	6:00	3:55
Previous Total This Year			262:03						
Total This Year			380:48						
Prior to this Year			0						
Total for P.A.A.			380:48						

	Month	Prior to No.
Military		
Other		
GRAND TOTAL		

Time flown for Pan
American Airways, Inc.
is certified as correct

O. F. Maxwell
O. F. MAXWELL
Acting Operations Manager.

Remarks:

During September 1942, pilot E. J. Frankiewicz logged 118 hours on the trans-Africa route.

Exhibit 3   167

Exhibit 3

PAA-Africa Operations Department Flight Summary
for the Month of April 1942

PILOTS TIME SUMMARY FOR APRIL 1942

SENIOR PILOTS

NAME	PRODUCTIVE HOURS FLOWN	TOTAL THIS YEAR	NUMBER MONTHS ACTIVE DUTY	AVERAGE FOR YEAR
Alison, R.F.	71:29	296:15	4	74:04
Blakely, H.H.	22:40	282:45	4	70:41
Bockman, C.E.	* 144:36	314:13	4	78:33
Bower, R.D.	62:42	301:42	4	75:25
Braun, R.A.	103:30	446:39	4	111:40
Buschmann, R.O.	25:40	25:40	New	–
Carstensen, B.S.	161:03	397:59	4	99:30
Collins, T.F.	81:03	312:59	4	78:15
Craig, D.S.	157:43	280:22	4	70:06
Davidov, W.H.	144:49	276:29	4	69:07
Davis, G.H.	78:21	265:49	4	66:27
Dixon, R.B.	–	208:33	4	52:08
Eknes, Orval	31:41	179:02	4	44:45
Eveland, I.W.	102:13	319:15	4	79:49
Fleury, P.A.	110:33	324:14	4	81:04
Francis, E.R.	99:58	304:42	4	76:11
Furr, G.C.	100:33	377:44	4	94:26
Glen, F.P.	113:06	156:09	4	39:02
Goyette, C.A.	76:41	327:44	4	81:56
Haley, R.E.	65:07	195:09	4	43:47
Heffner, C.B.	92:40	349:22	4	87:21
Heninger, J.H.	* 180:38	358:37	4	89:39
Herrman, G.R.	81:52	374:56	4	93:44
Hubbard, J.H.	67:45	279:09	4	69:47
Jones, H.H.	86:31	343:25	4	85:51
Kachler, Wm.	45:23	245:59	4	62:30
Kerns, V.L.	90:45	212:45	4	53:11
Kralgher, Geo.	114:55	245:42	4	61:26
Kristofferson, H.C.	67:22	205:31	4	51:23
Lanning, G.R.	112:05	307:23	4	76:52
Linenbach, C.F.	130:52	342:40	4	85:40
Looney, V.H.	140:25	296:41	4	74:10
Lovejoy, R.A.	80:52	142:29	2	71:15
Lund, C.J.	104:41	337:18	4	84:20
Mahoney, F.T.	83:45	277:52	4	69:28
Maxwell, G.F.	63:50	63:50	New	–
McKane, E.R.	65:04	267:04	4	66:46
Meyer, J.H.	129:34	293:27	4	73:22
Miller, C.L.	114:54	214:53	4	53:45
Moore, H.M.	126:04	341:40	4	85:25
Murphy, S.H.	62:55	254:40	4	63:40
Passage, J. T.	110:03	279:04	4	69:46
Perry, L. D.	74:25	270:46	4	67:42
Poplawski, H.R.	38.49	240.31	4	60.08

This extract from the Flight Summary indicates that the PAA-Africa pilots were flying many "productive hours," averaging 100 or more each month. The total for all senior pilots was 4,718, and cumulatively for the first four months, 14,254.

PAA-Africa Operations Department Flight Summary
for the Month of April 1942

Page 13 of 13 Pages
April, 1942

SUMMARY OF TWA OPERATIONS
OVER ROUTES OF
PAA-AFRICA, LTD.

MONTH OF APRIL 1942

STATION	TIME OF ARRIVAL		AIRCRAFT		REGISTRA-	TIME OF DEPARTURE		CAPT.
	Date	Time	Type	Number	TION NO.	Date	Time	
AOR			Boeing 307B		N-19907	4/2/42	0740	Chia-
MHL	4/2/42	1240	"	"		4/3/42	2122	ppino
						TO NAT		
AOR	4/3/42	1015	"	"	N-1940	4/4/42	1410	Terry
KRT	4/3/42	0840	"	"		4/5/42	1100	"
CAI	4/5/42	1700	"	"	"	4/7/42	1000	"
KRT	4/7/42	1600	"	"	"	4/7/42	1830	"
LCS	4/8/42	0900	"	"	"	4/8/42	1050	"
AOR	4/8/42	1210	"	"	"	4/9/42	1340	"
MHL	4/9/42	1800	"	"	"	4/9/42	2240	"
						TO NAT		
MHL	4/5/42	1131	"	"	N-19907	4/6/42	1200	Chia-
AOR	4/6/42	1637	"	"		4/7/42	1315	ppino
MHL	4/7/42	1750	"	"	"	4/7/42	2153	"
						TO NAT		
MHL	4/13/42	1246	"	"	N-19907	4/14/42	0925	Bowen
AOR	4/14/42	1447	"	"	"	4/17/42	0642	"
KAN	4/17/42	1150	"	"	"	4/17/42	2005	"
KRT	4/18/42	0615	"	"	"	4/18/42	0840	"
CAI	4/18/42	1440	"	"	"	4/22/42	1000	"
						TO KRT VIA ADEN		
KRT	4/25/42	1500	"	"	"	4/26/42	2115	"
AOR	4/27/42	1102	"	"	"			
MHL	4/23/42	1215	"	"	N-1940	4/23/42	1317	Rich-
AOR	4/23/42	1835	"	"	"	4/27/42	0711	ardson
KAN	4/27/42	1610	"	"	"	4/27/42	2040	"
KRT	4/28/42	0650	"	"	"	4/28/42	0917	"
CAI	4/28/42	1517	"	"	"			
MHL	4/27/42	1154	"	"	N-19909	4/27/42	1410	Hall
AOR	4/27/42	1900	"	"	"	4/30/42	0800	"
KAN	4/30/42	1210	"	"	"	4/30/42	1938	"
MHL	4/30/42	1446	"	"	N-19905	4/30/42	1732	Hanson
AOR	4/30/42	2100	"	"				

Another extract from the April 1942 operations summary shows that T.W.A.'s
Boeing 307 Stratoliners were being put to good use during the War flying across
Africa en route to the war zones.

Exhibit 4   169

Exhibit 4

Your Status in Militarization: letter, 2 September 1942

September 2, 1942

TO: Frankiewicz, E. J.

FROM: Assistant Manager, PAA-Africa, Ltd., Accra, Gold Coast.

SUBJECT: YOUR STATUS IN THE MILITARIZATION OF PAN AMERICAN AIRWAYS-AFRICA, LTD.

REFERENCE: Assistant Manager's general memorandum to all employees,
dated August 18, 1942.

Thorough consideration has been given to your present position with Pan
American Airways-Africa, Ltd., to your abilities, and to the position with
the Army of the United States in which you may be of greatest service when
the militarization of Pan American Airways-Africa, Ltd., is effected.

Following is the assignment which we are authorized to give you in the
Army of the United States or in the civilian employ* of the United States
Government, together with the terms of this assignment:

Position:*   1st LIEUTENANT

*If "civilian employee" is designated here, refer to supplementary
statement attached.

As announced in the memorandum of August 18th, the Executive, Operations,
Traffic, Medical, Communications and Meteorology Departments are to be
militarized as soon as practicable. If you are a member of one of these
departments, you must fill in the appropriate portion of the questionnaire
attached to this memorandum and return it to the Personnel Department,
Accra, within one week from the time of receipt.

Maintenance, Construction, Commissary and Personnel Departments are to be
militarized December 15, 1942, or sooner. All employees of these departments are requested to continue their duties until at least the date of
militarization, unless suitably replaced before. Meanwhile, if you are a
member of one of these departments, you must fill in the appropriate
portion of the questionnaire attached to this memorandum and return it to
the Personnel Department, Accra, within one week from the time of receipt.

John H. Yeomans

*This offer to join the Army was accompanied by a commitment form and the
pay-scales offered (e.g., $2,000 annual base pay for a 2nd Lieutenant).*

Exhibit 5

Pan American Airways System Identification Flight Pass

This was a typical flight pass issued by Pan American Airways System
(normally for an employee of Pan American Air Ferries, Inc.) for use on the
lines of Pan American Airways-Africa, Ltd.

Exhibit 6   171

Exhibit 6

Pan American Airways-Africa, Ltd. Air Express Tariff No. 1

BETWEEN / AND	Accra (Gold Coast) Per Kg.	Val.	Bathurst (Gambia) Per Kg.	Val.	Cairo (Egypt) Per Kg.	Val.
ACCRA, Gold Coast	....	....	8/2	1/	17/9	1/3
BATHURST, Gambia	8/2	1/	....	....	24/7	1/3
CAIRO, Egypt	17/9	1/3	24/7	1/3	....	....
EL FASHER, Anglo-Egyptian Sudan	10/10	1/	17/2	1/3	9/2	1/
EL GENEINA, Anglo-Egyptian Sudan	9/10	1/	16/	1/3	10/5	1/
EL OBEID, Anglo-Egyptian Sudan	12/5	1/	18/2	1/3	8/2	1/
FREETOWN, Sierra Leone	6/	7-½d.	2/9	7-½d.	22/7	1/3
FT. LAMY, French Equatorial Africa	7/5	1/	14/	1/	12/7	1/
■HARPER, Liberia	6/	7-½d.	6/	7-½d.	22/10	1/3
■KADUNA, Nigeria	4/2	7-½d.	11/2	1/	15/7	1/
KANO, Nigeria	5/	7-½d.	11/10	1/	14/9	1/
KHARTOUM, Anglo-Egyptian Sudan	12/7	1/	19/7	1/3	7/7	1/
LAGOS, Nigeria	1/10	5-½d.	9/	1/	16/7	1/3
MAIDUGURI, Nigeria	6/9	1/	13/5	1/	13/	1/
MARSHALL (Harbel Airp.), Liberia	4/5	7-½d.	4/5	7-½d.	21/2	1/3
MONROVIA (Fish'man Lake Airp.), Liberia	4/9	7-½d.	4/	7-½d.	21/7	1/3
■OSHOGBO, Nigeria	2/5	5-½d.	9/10	1/	16/	1/3
■SINO, Liberia	5/5	7-½d.	5/5	7-½d.	22/2	1/3
TAKORADI, Gold Coast	10d.	5-½d.	7/7	1/	18/5	1/3
■WADI HALFA, Anglo-Egyptian Sudan	14/9	1/	21/7	1/3	4/5	7-½d.

(Extract only) PAA-Africa offered air express service over the whole of its route from Bathurst, Gambia, to Cairo. Interestingly, all the rates and charges were in British shillings and pence. For example, the "8/2" for Accra–Bathurst would have been about $2.00 at the 1942 rate of exchange.

Exhibit 7

Pan American Airways Clipper Ticket

PAN AMERICAN AIRWAYS – AFRICA, LTD.

3958

PRIVATE CONTRACT CARRIER

TRIP PASS

Not Valid Unless Officially Stamped

IDENTIFICATION COUPON

NOT TRANSFERABLE

F

M......*FRANKIEWICZ*........

Form E

(Print Passenger's Name)

ACCOUNT......

ORIGINAL PLACE OF **LAGOS**
DEPARTURE......

ROUTE......

VIA......

FINAL
DESTINATION...... **ACCRA**

PASSAGE MUST
BE COMPLETED BY *MAY. 31st* ....19*43*.

This pass is issued by the Company as a private contract carrier.

Each of the annexed Flight Coupons, if and when officially stamped, and if presented attached hereto, will entitle the person named above, but no other person, to one passage between airports (including landing areas) at or in the vicinity of the points of departure and arrival thereunder, and also to transportation to and from such airports in local transfer services operated by or on behalf of the Company but only in the cases and to the extent that such transfer services are included within the fare regularly charged for passage between said points of departure and arrival, and as provided in the published tariffs, rules or regulations of the Company, subject, however, to the terms and conditions of such Flight Coupon(s), which are hereby made a part hereof, and subject also to the terms, conditions and provisions stated on pages 1, 2 and 3 of this Identification Coupon and to the published tariffs, rules and regulations of the Company, all of which are hereby made a part hereof and all of which shall be deemed, and are hereby made a part of each such Flight Coupon, and subject also to all applicable laws and governmental regulations, orders, demands and requirements.

Such terms, conditions, provisions, tariffs, rules and regulations shall be applicable to transportation under the annexed Flight Coupon(s) and to all services and operations related to such transportation performed or to be performed by, or with respect to which any liability might otherwise attach to, the Company, including (but without limitation) surface transportation (either land or water or both) and the receipt, custody, handling, checking, transfer, transportation and carriage of baggage (including both checked and unchecked baggage and both accompanied and unaccompanied baggage) transported or to be transported under any such Flight Coupon or under any baggage check of the Company.

Transportation under the annexed Flight Coupon(s) is subject to the rules relating to liability established by the Convention of Warsaw of 12th October, 1929 unless such transportation is not "international transportation" as defined in said Convention. As to transportation, carriage, services or

Continued on pages 2 and 3 of this Identification Coupon

War-time austerity demanded thrift. This was the ticket envelope, actual size, for a flight from Lagos to Accra in 1943.

Bibliography

BOOKS:

Bender, Marylin and Altschul, Selig, *The Chosen Instrument, Pan Am, Juan Trippe, The Rise and Fall of an American Entrepreneur.* New York: Simon and Schuster, 1982.

Brock, Horace, *Flying The Oceans.* Lunenburg, Vermont: The Stinehour Press, 1978.

_____, *More About Pan Am.* Lunenburg, Vermont: The Stinehour Press, 1980.

Christie, Carl A., *Ocean Bridge: The History of RAF Ferry Command.* Toronto and Buffalo: University of Toronto Press, 1995.

Cleveland, Reginald, *Air Transport at War.* New York and London: Harper & Brothers Publishers, 1946.

Curie, Eve, *Journey Among Warriors.* Garden City and New York: Doubleday, Doran and Co., Inc., 1943.

Daley, Richard, *An American Saga, Juan Trippe and His Pan Am Empire.* New York, NY: Random House, 1980.

Davies, R.E.G., *Pan Am: An Airline and Its Aircraft.* New York: Paladwr Press, 1992.

_____, *Airlines of the United States since 1914.* London: Putnam, 1972.

Dmitri, Ivan, *Flight To Everywhere.* New York: Whittlesey House, McGraw-Hill Book Company, Inc., 1944.

Ellsberg, Edward, *Under the Red Sea Sun*. New York: Dodd, Mead & Company, 1974.

Firestone Plantation Company, *Views In Liberia*. Firestone Plantation Company, 1937.

Fowle, Barry W. (ed.), *Builders and Fighters: U.S. Army Engineers In World War II*. United States Army Corps Of Engineers, Fort Belvoir, Virginia: Office of History, 1992.

Francillon, Rene J., *McDonnell Douglas Aircraft Since 1920*. London: Putnam, 1979.

Goutiere, Peter J., *Himalayan Rogue*. Paducah, Kentucky: Turner Publishing Company, 1994.

Higham, Robin, *Britain's Imperial Air Routes 1918–1939*. London: G.T. Foulis & Co. Ltd., 1960.

Masland, William M., *Through the Back Doors of the World in a Ship That Had Wings*. New York: Vantage Press,1984.

Ministry of Information, *Atlantic Bridge, The Official Account of R.A.F. Transport Command's Ocean Ferry*. London: His Majesty's Stationery Office, 1945.

Rowe, Captain Basil L., *Under My Wings*. New York: The Bobbs-Merrill Company, Inc., 1956.

Smith, Henry Ladd, *Airways Abroad: The Story of American World Air Routes*. Washington, D.C.: Smithsonian Institution Press, 1991.

Trippe, Betty Stettinius, *PAN AM'S FIRST LADY, The Diary of Betty Stettinius Trippe*. McLean, Virginia: Paladwr Press, 1996.

Turner, P. St. John, *Pictorial History Of Pan American World Airways*. Shepperton-Middlesex: Ian Allan Printing, Ltd., 1973.

Willkie, Wendell L., *One World*. New York: Simon and Schuster, 1943.

Wright, John C., Conlee, Robert A., and Nelson, Christopher R. *Flying With Sam Fox.* Air Command And Staff College, Air University, Maxwell, AFB, AL: Report Number 84-0565, 1984.

UNPUBLISHED PAPERS:

Gilmore, Voit, *African Report.* Internal Report, PAA-Africa, Ltd., January 1943.

Purcell, Edward T., *African Airline, A Study of Pan American Airways Operations in Africa, 1941–42.* M.A. Essay, New York, Columbia University, April 1946.

Ray, Deborah W., *Pan American Airways and the Trans-African Air Base Program of World War II.* Dissertation in the Department of History, New York University, 1973.

ARTICLES:

Bridgman, Leonard (ed.), *IntavaWorld.* London, S.W.I., International Aviation Associates, Artillery House, Artillery Row, Vol. 5, July 1943.

Hubler, Richard, *Pan Am Fights the Axis.* FLYING, June 1942, pp. 38+.

Josephson, Matthew, *Columbus of the Airways.* The Saturday Evening Post, September 11, 1943. pp. 22, 64, 67–70.

Lateiner, Major Robert, U.S. AAF (Medical Corps), *The Heroism of Burma's Dunkirk.* As told to Donald E. Keyhoe, New York, Readers Digest, November 1942.

Reynolds, Quentin, *These Are Your Sons.* Collier's, 15 May 1943.

Thomas, Don, *PAA-Africa: Victory Over the White Man's Grave.* Journal of the American Aviaton Historical Society, Fall, 1991.

Wharton, Don, *Our New Life Line to the East.* Saturday Evening Post, August 1, 1942. pp.19, 65–66.

PAN AMERICAN AIRWAYS PERIODICALS:

Africa News Letter, Pan American Airways–Africa, Ltd., Chrysler Building, New York City, March 31–September 15, 1942.

New Horizons, Pan American Airways, Chrysler Building, New York City, January–December 1942.

Index

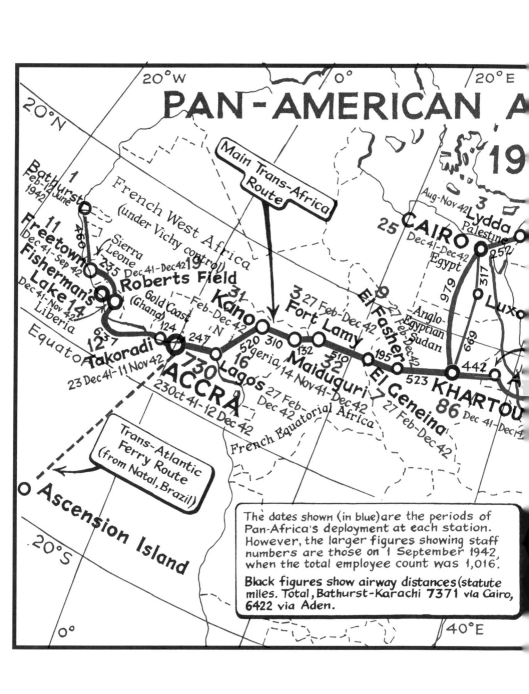

PAN-AMERICAN A

19

Main Trans-Africa Route

20°W · 0° · 20°E

20°N

Bathurst
Feb-12 June
1942
1

French West Africa
(under Vichy control)

11
Freetown
Dec 41-Sep 42
235
Sierra
Leone
Dec 41-Dec42 19
7

Fisherman's
Lake 14
Dec 41-Nov 42
Liberia

Roberts Field
Gold Coast
(Ghana) 124

Kano 31
Feb-Dec 42
Nigeria, 14 Nov 41-Dec42
520 310

Fort Lamy
3 27 Feb-Dec 42

El Fasher 9
27 Feb-Dec 42

25 CAIRO
Dec 41-Dec 42
Egypt

Aug-Nov 42 3
Lydda
Palestine

252

Luxo

317

979

Anglo-
Egyptian
Sudan
Dec 41-Dec 42

669

Equator
12

Takoradi 637
23 Dec 41-11 Nov 42

247
730
16
Lagos
27 Feb-
Dec 42

Maiduguri 32
27 Feb-
Dec 42

132 510
195

El Geneina 7
27 Feb-Dec 42

442

523

KHARTOU
86 Dec 41-Dec 4

ACCRA
23 Oct 41-12 Dec 42

French Equatorial Africa

Trans-Atlantic
Ferry Route
(from Natal, Brazil)

Ascension Island

20°S

0°

40°E

The dates shown (in blue) are the periods of
Pan-Africa's deployment at each station.
However, the larger figures showing staff
numbers are those on 1 September 1942
when the total employee count was 1,016.

Black figures show airway distances (statute
miles. Total, Bathurst-Karachi 7371 via Cairo,
6422 via Aden.